Knowing Me
Knowing You

Classroom activities to develop learning strategies
and stimulate conversation

Jim Wingate

Published by

DELTA Publishing
39 Alexandra Road
Addlestone
Surrey KT15 2PQ

and

ENGLISH TEACHING *professional*
First Person Publishing Limited
15 Baldwyn Gardens
London W3 6HJ

© Jim Wingate 2000

First published 2000

ISBN 0 953 30983 5

Edited by Susan Norman and Mike Burghall

Book design and front cover by Hugh L'Estrange at
Saffire Press

Illustrations from DeskGallery, courtesy of
Zedcor Inc., Tucson, Arizona, USA

Printed in England by Hillman Printers (Frome) Ltd

Acknowledgements

The author would like to acknowledge the following
sources for the inspiration for some of the activities:

Alice Miller *For Your Own Good* Virago 1987 for the
activity 'Toxic Teaching'

David Nunan *Getting started with learner-centred
teaching* in ENGLISH TEACHING *professional* Issue Four for
the activity 'Learning English'

Susan Norman for the activities 'Good Student, Better
Student' and 'Future Dreams'

*Other acknowledgements have been made in the relevant
Teaching Notes.*

ENGLISH TEACHING *professional* (ET*p*) is a quarterly magazine for
teachers of English worldwide, publishing articles on practical
methodology and personal and professional development. ET*p*
provides the fresh ideas and renewed enthusiasm that every
classroom teacher needs.

For more information about ENGLISH TEACHING *professional*
please contact:

ENGLISH TEACHING *professional*
Tech West House
10 Warple Way
London W3 0UE
England

Tel +44 (0) 20 8762 9600
Fax +44 (0) 20 8749 6916
Email etp@etprofessional.com
Web www.etprofessional.com

**Teaching English is your profession
ENGLISH TEACHING *professional* is your magazine**

DELTA Publishing aims to provide teachers of English – wherever
they are and whatever their teaching situation – with innovative,
creative, practical resource materials to help them in their everyday
teaching tasks.

For further information and a copy of the latest DELTA
Publishing catalogue, please contact:

Eileen Fryer
DELTA PUBLISHING
39 Alexandra Road
Addlestone
Surrey KT15 2PQ
England

Tel +44 (0)1932 854776
Fax +44 (0)1932 849528
Email delta@deltabooks.co.uk
Web www.deltapublishing.co.uk

Creative materials for creative teachers

CONTENTS

✸ *These are free-standing activities designed to get the teacher and the students thinking about themselves in a new way. They can be done at any time in any order – just for fun!*

INTRODUCTION

Aims

For students to:

- talk, especially about the most motivating subject of all – themselves
- find out about their individual thinking styles
- discover their preferred methods of learning
- take responsibility for their own learning, rather than blaming their books (or their teachers)
- improve their fluency
- expand their vocabulary
- practise reading and listening

For teachers to

- discover more about their individual thinking styles – and those of their students
- find out their preferred methods of learning and of teaching

… so that they can teach the individual students in their classes more effectively.

Contents

Through a variety of activities, such as worksheets, questionnaires, students are encouraged to find out about their natural thinking styles and preferred learning methods, all through the medium of English.

You, the teacher, have the same fascinating opportunities for self-discovery, and for developing your teaching skills as you work through the exercises with your students.

Activities range from a serious analysis of how students learn, based on Neuro-Linguistic Programming (NLP) and Multiple Intelligences theory, through to fun 'pop psychology' quizzes.

Levels and ages

These lessons have been used with teenagers at early intermediate level, and at all higher levels with both adults and teenagers. Most can be adapted for use with particular groups. Each activity is graded for language level in the relevant Teaching Notes:

✳	Early intermediate and above
✳✳	Middle intermediate and above
✳✳✳	High intermediate and above

How to use this book

- Make one copy of the photocopiable worksheet and do each task yourself first before you use it with students. This will help you gain maximum personal benefit from the activities, as well as giving you an understanding of how your students might react, and what language they might need to use.
- Read through all the information in the Teaching Notes for the activity.
- Write on the page you have photocopied any vocabulary you think your students might need, or any changes you want to make.
- Make a copy for each student.
- Follow the instructions under 'Method' on the page of Teaching Notes or exploit the activity as you see fit.
- *Alternatively, to save on photocopying, you could copy the pages onto overhead transparencies and ask students to write or draw on blank paper.*
- Explain to students that the principal purpose of the activities is to stimulate conversation. They will have the chance to express their opinions in the conversations, and it is up to them how much or how little they want to reveal about themselves to others.

Which activities do I do first?

The sections and the individual activities can be done in any order, *except* that the activities within the sections INTELLIGENCE, SENSORY LEARNING and THE BRAIN are designed to be done in the given order. After a few months, some students may want to do some of the exercises again – perhaps they have changed and developed, or they have more language, or they have developed greater self-awareness. Why not give them a choice of repeat activities (eg one out of three)?

 'Pop psychology' activities (marked with this symbol) are relatively quick and easy. Since they are self-standing, they can be used at any time as a 'filler' or to energise students between more serious activities.

Language input

Students will learn a lot of vocabulary receptively through reading and listening, driven by their need to understand the content and what to do. Sometimes relevant vocabulary is given on the worksheet, or students are specifically asked to complete language enhancement activities (eg word sort). Other possibilities are:

- Giving students vocabulary immediately when they need it – on a slip of paper or by whispering in their ears or writing the phrase they need on the board
- Noticing language needs during the activities and following up with more formal presentation and practice in a later lesson
- Introducing vocabulary or phrases by using them yourself for students to learn receptively

- Leaving time at the end of each activity for students to note down useful language.

You can also introduce different grammatical structures to be the focus of the activities.

Keeping students speaking English

- Change pairs or groups during the lesson.
- Each person chooses an English name and an English personality for themselves.
- Each group has a monitor whose job it is to keep the language English.
- Have notices on the desks and walls *'Let's speak English', 'English only'.*
- You are the 'resource person' with a different assistant in each lesson. The assistant goes round listening and tells you words or sentences the learners say in the mother tongue. You tell the assistant the English and he/she tells the students, while you write the English onto a big piece of paper for all to see in the next lesson. The English they need accumulates lesson by lesson.
- Remind students that this is a fun, and relatively painless, way to learn and practise English Although you know that it is somewhat ridiculous to ask them to speak to their friends in English, if they are all prepared to 'play the game of speaking English', then their English will improve much more quickly.

Always remember that there is a magic element in the classroom making all the activities meaningful and productive – you!

Have fun!

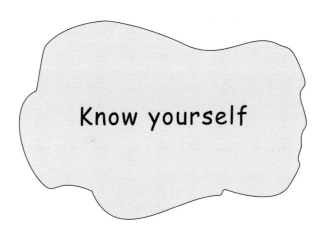

Know yourself

Aim

This free-standing activity can be done at any time. It might give students insights into themselves, but its main aim is to stimulate interest and discussion and to get students used to talking about themselves.

To the teacher

Before you look at the Notes, make one copy of the questionnaire and do the activity fully yourself – including sorting the animals and adjectives! Then read the Notes (opposite) and interpret what you've written.

What did you learn about yourself? Did you enjoy doing the activity? Do you agree with the interpretation? And the reasons?

Decide how to exploit the activity most effectively with your students.

Method

1   If you want to add anything to the worksheet, make one copy first, make your changes and then make a copy for each student.

2   Students work in pairs or small groups to sort the words and add more words to each group, using dictionaries if necessary. (Putting the words in alphabetical order will aid the checking process and will also help students learn them.) Share the additional words with the whole class. Check the meanings of any words students still don't know.

   This preparation gives students the opportunity to think about lots of different animals and adjectives and gives them words in English.

3   It is important that students do the Favourite Animals activity individually. Control the speed of the activity by reading aloud each question in turn and making sure everyone has finished before moving on to the next question.

4   In small groups, students compare their choices and think about what they might mean.

5   Tell students what each question 'means', giving them time between each to talk. In their groups they compare what they have written and discuss whether they think it's true.

Optional follow up

Students write about themselves using the adjectives in this exercise, eg in a letter to a penfriend.

Level ✳

Notes

- Your favourite animal = your self-image = how you want others to see you.

- Your second favourite animal = your image = how other people do see you.

- Your third favourite animal = you = how you really are.

- The adjectives describing your least favourite animals are the things you don't like about yourself.

Although it seems unlikely that this activity could have any validity, it is often surprisingly accurate. People usually like and dislike in others (and in animals) things they like and dislike in themselves.

The first animal and adjectives you think of will be the ones closest to the surface of your mind – the way you present yourself to others. You will have to think a bit harder about your second animal and adjectives – and most people will see through your surface impression to the 'you' underneath. You will really have to dig more deeply to find a third animal and adjectives – which describes the hidden, more private you. By the time you are thinking about things you don't like, you will probably be quite spontaneous – and have fairly strong views, after all those 'nice' adjectives.

WORD SORT

Sort these words into two groups: animals and adjectives, then add three more words to each group.

> graceful · fly · old · enormous · bee · ant · courageous · happy · butterfly
> quiet · beetle · warm · worm · snake · beautiful · bat · mouse · funny · rat
> courageous · stupid · hamster · sad · guinea-pig · gerbil · slow · cat · dog
> smooth · horse · crazy · sensible · dolphin · elephant · obedient · crocodile
> hard · eagle · ugly · robin · lion · cuddly · tiger · panther · rough · strong
> leopard · shy · wolf · tame · whale · weak · free · cow · wild · sheep · loving
> helpful · goat · cute · angry · hen · brave · duck · peaceful · goose · turkey
> fierce · bear · hateful · panda · cold · koala · fearful · fish · donkey · timid
> dinosaur · monkey · tiny · young · gorilla · friendly · chimpanzee · unfriendly
> penguin · fast · wise · stubborn · seahorse · shark · noisy · patient
> jellyfish · independent · soft

FAVOURITE ANIMALS

Answer the following questions in order. It is important that you answer each question completely before you move on to the next. Once you have written something, do not change it. Use different adjectives to describe each animal.

A   What is your favourite animal? _____

Write four adjectives to describe your favourite animal.

1 _____   2 _____

3 _____   4 _____

B   What is your second favourite animal? _____

Write four adjectives to describe your second favourite animal.

1 _____   2 _____

3 _____   4 _____

C   What is your third favourite animal? _____

Write four adjectives to describe your third favourite animal.

1 _____   2 _____

3 _____   4 _____

D   What is your least favourite animal? _____

Write four adjectives to describe your least favourite animal.

1 _____   2 _____

3 _____   4 _____

Aim

This activity is best done near the beginning of a year or a term. It helps students realise that their attitudes, their approaches and their interests are an important part of their learning success. It can also help you plan the sort of work to which students will be committed, and it shows them that you are interested in their opinions.

To the teacher

Make a copy of the worksheet for yourself and fill in what you expect your students to answer. Consider how the ideas correspond to your preferred teaching patterns.

Decide how to exploit the activity most effectively with your students and make a note of any other ideas which you might want to introduce at the discussion stage.

Method

1   If you want to add anything to the worksheet, make one copy first, make your changes and then make a copy for each student.

2   Make a large master sheet of the questions for the OHP or on a wall poster.

3   Students complete the questionnaire working individually.

4   In pairs or small groups, they compare and discuss their results.

5   Onto the large sheet, collect everyone's results. Add up the total class score for each statement.

6   Discuss each area from the questionnaire with the class. Three volunteers note the significant things people say.

7   While the volunteers prepare a report on the discussion, the rest of the class divides into small groups and they discuss anything else they think is relevant to their lessons and their learning. One student from each group reports back to the class.

And/or

Five groups each take responsibility for producing the results of the questionnaire visually, perhaps as a pie chart or a bar chart.

8   Everyone (including the teacher) sits quietly and considers all the information which has been collected.

9   Discuss with the class the comparison between your predictions and what they actually want. Say that you will plan the term's work and present it to them in the next lesson.

10   In the next lesson, explain to the students your plan for the term's work, showing clearly how you have taken into account their wishes, and where (and for what reasons) you have had to deviate.

Level   ✳

Pie chart

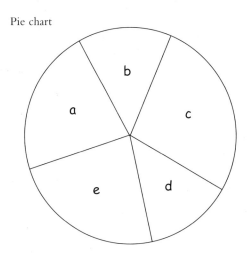

Bar chart

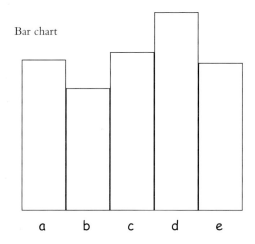

What's your attitude to learning English? Circle a number according to the following key:

(1) I don't like this at all (2) I don't like this very much (3) This is OK (4) I quite like this (5) I like this very much

Language

The following language might be useful. Add any other words or phrases you would like to remember.

I enjoy working alone.

I really like/don't like reading.

I don't really like doing grammar exercises.

I prefer talking to writing.

I want the teacher to correct my mistakes.

Topics

In my English class, I would like to study topics ...

a)	about me, my feelings, attitudes, beliefs	1	2	3	4	5
b)	from other subjects, eg psychology, literature	1	2	3	4	5
c)	from popular culture, eg music, film	1	2	3	4	5
d)	about life in English-speaking countries	1	2	3	4	5
e)	about current affairs and controversial issues	1	2	3	4	5

Methods

In my English class, I would like to learn by ...

a)	discussions in pairs and groups, problem-solving	1	2	3	4	5
b)	formal language study, eg from a textbook	1	2	3	4	5
c)	listening to explanations from the teacher	1	2	3	4	5
d)	listening to tapes, playing games, watching videos	1	2	3	4	5
e)	reading and using texts	1	2	3	4	5

Out of class

To improve my English out of class, I like to ...

a)	have conversations with native English speakers	1	2	3	4	5
b)	study grammar/vocabulary with self-study books	1	2	3	4	5
c)	practise English with my friends	1	2	3	4	5
d)	watch TV, listen to the radio, read in English	1	2	3	4	5
e)	collect interesting/puzzling examples of English	1	2	3	4	5
f)	use English on the internet	1	2	3	4	5

Assessment

To find out how much my English is improving, I want ...

a)	the teacher to assess my written work	1	2	3	4	5
b)	the teacher to correct my mistakes in class	1	2	3	4	5
c)	to have regular tests in class	1	2	3	4	5
d)	to check my progress and correct my mistakes	1	2	3	4	5
e)	to be corrected by my fellow students	1	2	3	4	5
f)	to try using the language in real-life situations	1	2	3	4	5

LANGUAGE AREAS

This year I most want to improve my ...

a)	listening	1	2	3	4	5	d) writing	1	2	3	4	5
b)	speaking	1	2	3	4	5	e) grammar	1	2	3	4	5
c)	reading	1	2	3	4	5	f) pronunciation	1	2	3	4	5

Aim

This activity helps students consider and assess their natural style of working and interacting with others.

To the teacher

Make a copy of the worksheet for yourself. Grade each list 1-6. Mentally explain to someone else why you have graded your lists in this way. Notice the language you want to use.

Pay particular attention to the education list. What is your view of education? Be prepared to state your views on education, if the students ask.

Decide how to exploit the activity most effectively with your students.

Method

1   If you want to add anything to the worksheet, make one copy first, make your changes and then make a copy for each student. Tell them that the purpose of the activity is to practise the language of agreement, disagreement and persuasion.

2   Students grade each list individually and then choose one list to compare with a partner. Ask them to persuade their partner to accept their view. Pairs then agree a joint list and add a seventh item. (Any pairs who finish early can discuss one of the other lists.)

3   When this first part of the activity is finished, ask students to think about their natural way of working. *How* did they work with one another? Ask some or all of the questions on the right.

   The activity is set up to encourage students' natural competitiveness (and the competitiveness encouraged by most school systems). However, you might like to discuss the idea of co-operation when students are working together on projects.

4   Students follow the instructions for the education list. When they have compared their opinions in small groups, a representative of each group reports back to the rest of the class.

5   Discuss the education section as a whole class. What do they think the role of education is? Why do they go to school? In an ideal world, what would school be like?

   Here are some additional items you might offer to the class to add to the education list:

   To enhance learners' self esteem
   To teach learners to think
   To prepare learners for life

Level ✳

Questions

- *How did you order the six items?*
- *How did you persuade your partner (or allow yourself to be persuaded)?*
- *How did you agree a seventh item together?*
- *How did you prepare the report?*
- *How did you report it? Who spoke? Why?*
- *Did you work well with others?*
- *Did you find it easy to come to an agreement?*
- *Who was the leader in your pair? And in your group?*
- *Who spoke the most? And the least?*
- *How much did you speak and how much did you listen?*
- *How easy was it to accept another person's point of view?*
- *How could you do the activity better another time?*

Language

The following language might be useful. Add any other words or phrases you would like to remember.

Perhaps, but have you thought about ... ?

I think the most important thing is ...

So do I.

I don't agree.

... is more important than ...

To my mind ...

In my opinion ...

As far as I'm concerned ...

What about ... ?

We could add ...

Well done!

That's a good idea.

I think I prefer my/your/his/her idea.

PARTY
- [ ] Drinks
- [ ] Food
- [ ] Music
- [ ] Dancing
- [ ] Conversation
- [ ] People
- [ ] _____

FRIEND
- [ ] Loyal
- [ ] Keeps my secrets
- [ ] Listens well
- [ ] Sense of humour
- [ ] Things in common
- [ ] Attractive
- [ ] _____

ROCK MUSIC
- [ ] Rhythm
- [ ] Melody
- [ ] Words of the song
- [ ] Harmony and counterpoint
- [ ] Style of the singer
- [ ] Message for the listeners
- [ ] _____

HOLIDAY
- [ ] Place
- [ ] Weather
- [ ] People you go with
- [ ] Activities
- [ ] Meeting new people
- [ ] Social life
- [ ] _____

♦ Put the items in the four lists above in the order you think is best, writing 1 against the most important, 2 against the second most important ... down to 6 for the least important.

♦ Choose one of the lists and explain to your partner why you put it in this order. Listen to your partner's opinions. Decide on an order for the list that you both agree on. Add a seventh item to the list.

♦ Join with another pair and discuss your lists. Explain your own point of view. Try to get other people to agree with you.

The purpose of EDUCATION
- [ ] To develop learners' bodies
- [ ] To develop imagination and creativity
- [ ] To prepare learners for exams
- [ ] To give learners information
- [ ] To prepare learners for jobs
- [ ] To teach discipline and good behaviour
- [ ] To keep learners happy
- [ ] _____
- [ ] _____

I think, therefore I am

♦ Put the above list into the order that you think is best, adding more items if you would like to.

♦ Explain your list to your partner. Listen to your partner's opinions. Decide on a list and an order that you agree on.

♦ In small groups, discuss your views on education. Prepare a short report to present to the rest of the class.

Aim

This activity makes explicit students' understanding of what makes a teacher more or less effective.

To the teacher

Make a copy of the questionnaire and do it yourself. Before, during and after doing the activity with students, consider your own role as a teacher and note things you could do to improve your teaching.

If any of the comments about bad teachers seem to apply to you (or seem to be directed at you), try to remain calm and receptive (outwardly, at least!) and consider positive ways in which you can improve as a teacher. The more open and honest you can be with your students in this process, the better your relationship with them is likely to be and the more likely they are to accept suggestions from you about changes in their own behaviour.

Decide how to exploit the activity most effectively with your students.

Method

1   If you want to add anything to the worksheet, make one copy first, make your changes, and then make a copy for each student.

2   Students individually write three things they think good teachers do and three things bad teachers do.

3   In small groups, students share their ideas. Each group reports back to the class.

4   In their groups, students complete the instructions for being a good or a bad teacher, eg *You should be friendly. You must always shout at your students.*

   Instructions can be written in the imperative, or using the language of advice (eg *should*) or instruction (eg *must, must not, need not*).

5   Everyone reads the different sets of instructions. (Leave the instructions on desks and students move round to read other people's ideas.)

6   Students work in new groups and write down the possible advantages and disadvantages for students of having a good or bad teacher. (There may be advantages for some people in having a bad teacher – it might make them more determined to succeed, it might make them decide to become a teacher to help other people learn, etc.)

7   When all the groups have finished, everyone reads all the lists.

8   Read out the information about the research into good and bad teachers and have a general class discussion about good teaching.

Level   ✳

Notes

After 3700 hours of research in 550 elementary and secondary schools, two researchers called Aspy and Roebuck found that the best teachers had three things in common. The crucial things were not whether the teacher was 'traditional' or 'liberal', 'well organised' or 'spontaneous', 'friendly' or 'professional'. Nor were they to do with their teaching styles or qualifications. They were:

Transparency – they weren't wearing a mask, there was no façade, no pretence, they were 'people' before they were 'teachers'.

Prizing their learners – they gave unconditional, non-judgmental care to the students (not prizing their behaviour, but prizing them as people).

Showing empathy – they understood (and showed that they understood) the inner world of the student.

When a teacher has these three qualities, students show an average increase in their measurable intelligence of 10%. When a teacher does not have these qualities, students show an average decrease in their measurable intelligence of 10%. The difference in measurable intelligence between students with a good teacher and students with a bad teacher is therefore 20%! If the students are 10 years old, with a good teacher they function like 11 year olds, with a bad teacher they function like nine year olds. That's a two-year difference!

When a teacher is good at being transparent, prizing the students, and showing empathy, the students become more adept at problem solving, they become more creative, they have fewer discipline problems and fewer absences from lessons, they initiate more positive behaviour in the classroom (ie they take more responsibility for their own learning and rely less on the teacher), and they have a more positive self concept (higher self esteem).

Language

The following language might be useful. Add any other words or phrases you would like to remember.

Fair/unfair

Impartial

Knowledgeable

Friendly

A good teacher should (listen to students).

A bad teacher never (sets homework).

It might be an advantage if a teacher is lazy, because …

You should/shouldn't (shout at students).

You must/mustn't be friendly.

✔ GOOD TEACHERS

Think of good teachers you know. Write down three things that make them good.

_____

_____

_____

✘ BAD TEACHERS

Think of bad teachers you know. Write down three things that make them bad.

_____

_____

_____

INSTRUCTIONS

✔ How to be a good teacher	✘ How to be a bad teacher
_____	_____
_____	_____
_____	_____
_____	_____
_____	_____
_____	_____

What are the possible advantages and disadvantages for students who have good and bad teachers?

ADVANTAGES	DISADVANTAGES
✔ Good teachers	
_____	_____
_____	_____
✘ Bad teachers	
_____	_____
_____	_____
_____	_____

Aim

This activity helps students make explicit for themselves what it means to be a good student – as a first step to becoming one.

To the teacher

Make a copy of the worksheet and do it yourself as 'you' – yourself as a student.

What do you learn about your own ways of studying? When you teach, do you take account of people who study in the same way as you do? What about people who learn better when they study in different ways?

What do you think your students might write in answer to these questions?

Decide how to exploit the activity most effectively with your students.

Method

1   If you want to add anything to the worksheet, make one copy first, make your changes, and then make a copy for each student.

2   Read aloud each of the first four statements in turn and give students time to write their answers individually.

3   In small groups, students share their ideas and then discuss how they can help each other become better students.

4   Individually, students write the skill they can teach and the skill they would like to learn. Students get together in pairs or small groups to teach and learn these study skills.

Level ✳

Notes

This activity depends on the students knowing what they need to do in order to study – and they do know! If students decide for themselves what they need to do, rather than being told by the teacher what they must do, they are much more likely to take responsibility for their learning.

Students are more likely to be committed to this activity if they have done 'Good Teacher, Bad Teacher', Activity 4.

Language

The following language might be useful. Add any other words or phrases you would like to remember.

Attentive

Hard-working

Considerate

Lazy

Disruptive

Listen to the teacher

Study out of class

Help my friends

I never do more than I'm asked to do.

I leave everything till the last minute.

✔ GOOD STUDENTS

Think of good students you know (or have known). Write down three things that make them good students.

1 _____

2 _____

3 _____

✘ BAD STUDENTS

Think of bad students you know (or have known). Write down three things that made them bad students.

1 _____

2 _____

3 _____

YOU

Think about yourself as a student. Write five things you are good at and five things you could do better.

Five ways in which I am a good student.

1 _____

2 _____

3 _____

4 _____

5 _____

Five things I could do to be a better student.

1 _____

2 _____

3 _____

4 _____

5 _____

Describe one skill you have that you would like to teach to others.

_____

Describe one skill that you would like to learn from someone else.

_____

Aim

Level ✳ ✳

The aim of this activity is to get students thinking and talking about the roles of teachers and learners.

To the teacher

Make a copy of the worksheet and complete it yourself, bearing in mind your own experiences as a student and your role (or roles) as a teacher.

What do you learn about your own attitudes to teaching and learning? Are your beliefs evident in your actual day-to-day teaching?

Decide how to exploit the activity most effectively with your students.

Method

1 Prepare one copy of the worksheet for each student.

2 Start by brainstorming adjectives and behaviour which could be attributed to bad schools and teachers – the ones which actually inhibit students' learning.

3 Give copies of the worksheet to students. They check their understanding of the 'toxic teaching rules' and formulate a sentence meaning the opposite. The emphasis is on an opposite 'meaning' rather than simply producing an opposite grammatical form.

4 Check with the whole class any different opposites they have generated.

5 In pairs, students discuss and write down their own beliefs. (Individuals might have slightly different beliefs – in which case, they write down both.)

6 Students then allocate a percentage to their own beliefs, in terms of taking a position between the two extremes, and mark it on the chart at the bottom of the worksheet. (If they disagree, they can take an average figure, or just agree to differ on their personal worksheets.)

7 On the board draw a copy of the 'Toxic Rules' chart from the worksheet. Taking each question in turn, mark the question number for each person's percentage figure when they call it out. Students discuss what the percentages mean. Encourage debate between pairs with widely different views. Other students listen and comment.

8 Add your own opinions to the chart and justify your beliefs if necessary.

9 Draw up a class list of rules for teaching that you can all agree on. Give your rules a title.

WRITE the opposite of these 'rules' for toxic teaching – and then decide what you believe. If the 'toxic teaching rules' are 0% and the opposites are 100%, write in a percentage to represent your beliefs.

	Toxic Rules	Opposites	My beliefs	%
1	The teacher is always right.			
2	Teachers deserve respect because they are teachers.			
3	Learners deserve no respect because they are learners.			
4	Teachers can eliminate anger and hatred by forbidding them.			
5	Obeying the teacher makes students strong.			
6	High self-esteem in a student stops them learning.			
7	Low self-esteem in a student is helpful to others in the class.			
8	Love of any kind has no place in the classroom.			
9	The teacher's job is to tell students what to feel and think.			
10	It is the students' fault if the teacher is angry.			
11	It is the students' fault if they do not learn.			
12	Students should thank the teacher (even if they are not grateful).			

Toxic Rules   Opposites

0   10   20   30   40   50   60   70   80   90   100

Aim

This free-standing activity can be done at any time to get students thinking and talking about their values.

To the teacher

Before you read the Notes, read the story and put the characters in order according to who you think was most and least to blame. Then read the Notes (opposite) and consider whether they actually reflect your beliefs and values.

Decide how to exploit the activity most effectively with your students. How do you think they will rank the characters?

Different people can hold different opinions quite strongly, but you may find that if your students are all of a similar age and background, they may quite quickly be largely in agreement. The activity allows for this, but you might like to prepare some ideas of your own, both attacking and in defence of each character, so that you can offer a provocative viewpoint.

Method

1 If you want to add anything to the worksheet, make one copy first, make your changes and then make a copy for each student.

2 Students read the story (or you read the story to them as a listening comprehension) and rank the characters according to who they think was most and least to blame. At this stage, they should make their decisions individually.

3 Students work in small groups to discuss their opinions and try to reach a group decision.

4 In different small groups, students take turns to roleplay the characters, who are interviewed by the other group members.

5 After hearing all the different opinions, students write their final personal ranking of the characters.

6 Read the different meanings to the class.

7 Students discuss whether they agree with the interpretations, and whether these do reflect their values. They might also discuss how much they were influenced by the opinions of others.

Optional follow up

Students write a newspaper report about the death of the woman on the bridge – or produce a TV or radio report – including interviews with the four 'survivors'. Remember that they will need to 'flesh them out' into real people with all the shades of grey that actually accompany a moral problem like this. This could lead to interesting work on describing someone's character rather than simply their appearance.

Level ✳

Notes

This story was given to undergraduates at Oxford University who were studying law. The aim was to show them that different people with the same information can come to very different conclusions about who is to blame in a hypothetical situation.

The suggestion is that your list reveals your values. The person you blame most for the woman's death (the person you gave as number 1) represents the attribute you value least. The person you blame least represents the attribute you value most.

The attributes associated with the characters are:

The woman   = individual choice

The husband = marriage

The lover   = sexual freedom

The soldier = law and order

The boatman = money

Language

The following language might be useful. Add any other words or phrases you would like to remember.

It was his fault.

It was her own fault.

He/she was the most to blame.

He was innocent.

Everyone is responsible for his or her own actions.

He was only doing his job.

He/she shouldn't have done that.

If he/she had/hadn't (done that), this wouldn't have happened.

The Bridge

A woman lived with her husband in a town beside a river. One day her husband went away for three months.

While her husband was away, the woman took a lover, who lived across the bridge on the other side of the river.

One day, while she was with her lover, the woman heard that her husband was coming home. She left her lover and tried to cross the bridge. But now there was a soldier on the bridge. The soldier said, 'Stop. I have orders that no-one must cross the bridge. If you try to cross the bridge, I will shoot you.'

Near the bridge was a boat. The woman told the boatman she needed to cross the river. The boatman said he would take her across the river if she paid him $100.

The woman didn't have $100, so she asked her lover to give her the money, but he refused.

The woman tried to cross the bridge.

The soldier shot her dead.

There are five characters in the story. Who do you think was most to blame for the woman's death? Who was least to blame?

· Grade the characters in the 'First List' column below with the numbers 1 – 5: 1 = most to blame, 5 = least to blame.

· In small groups, discuss your personal lists and agree a 'Group List'.

· Take turns in roleplaying the characters while the rest of the group ask questions. (To interview the woman, you can have a séance with the dead!)

· After hearing all the different opinions, write your own personal decision about who was most and least to blame for the woman's death in the 'Final List' column. Is it different from your first list?

	FIRST LIST	GROUP LIST	FINAL LIST
Woman	_____	_____	_____
Husband	_____	_____	_____
Lover	_____	_____	_____
Soldier	_____	_____	_____
Boatman	_____	_____	_____

Aim

This activity introduces the different specialisations of the two hemispheres of the brain to help students understand their preferred learning style.

To the teacher

Make one copy of the worksheet and do the task yourself. Compare your answer with the Notes.

How much did you already know about the specialisations of the two sides of the brain? How much do you take them into account in your teaching?

Decide how to exploit this activity most effectively with your students.

Method

1 Make one copy of the worksheet for each student.

2 In groups, students work out the opposites (using a dictionary if necessary).

3 They indicate whether they think they naturally prefer to use right-brain skills, left-brain skills or a balanced combination.

4 Ask them which type of thinking is traditionally favoured by schools and state education systems (the left). What implications does this have for teachers and learners?

5 Traditionally in western culture and western education systems, left-brain ways of thinking are considered superior, and right-brain ways are considered inferior. Men are supposed to think with their left brains, and women with their right brains! Right-brain ways of thinking are generally considered to be 'talents', such as being a good musician, dancer, etc. Students can discuss these points in small groups or as a whole class.

6 Read out the information about the left and right brain. Ask them to talk about times they have been 'very left-brained' or 'very right-brained'. Groups report back any clear examples.

Level ✳✳✳

Notes

The most effective way to use your brain is to use the appropriate part of the brain for the appropriate task, eg counting is sequential, linear, digital and logical, so people who find this easy are using the left brain; imagery is synthetic, analogic and spatial, so people who like to daydream are using their right brain.

The most effective thinkers use both sides of their brains. Albert Einstein as a young man saw mathematical problems that no-one had been able to solve. He used his right brain intuitively to imagine the answers, as spatial, non-rational visions. Then he used his left brain logically to work step-by-step from the problems to prove the answers. If he hadn't imagined the answers (with his right brain), he couldn't have started on the problems. If he hadn't used his left brain, he couldn't have proved the answers.

On the first day of a new course or in your first day of a new job, you have to be in the correct place at the correct time, ready with the correct things, to do the tasks in the correct way. That's very left-brain, and your right brain gets hungry. So when you get home, you put your watch aside, say 'don't talk to me', and just daydream or fantasise with no words. That's very right-brain!

On the first day of a holiday, you don't worry about time or place. You just lie on the beach or in bed and enjoy relaxing and letting your mind wander. That's very right-brain, and your left brain gets hungry. After a while, your left brain demands you do a crossword puzzle or read a book, etc.

Answers

1-G   2-F   3-A   4-C   5-B   6-I   7-E   8-D   9-H

The part of your brain concerned with higher thinking skills, the cerebral cortex, is divided into two hemispheres – the left and the right. Broadly speaking, the two sides of the brain have different specialisations. Match the specialisations on the left with their corresponding opposites on the right.

Left brain

1 Verbal
Using words to name, describe and define

2 Analytic
Figuring things out step-by-step and part-by-part

3 Symbolic
Using a symbol to stand for something, eg 👁 stands for 'eye', '+' stands for 'addition'

4 Abstract
Taking out a small bit of information and using it to represent the whole picture

5 Temporal
Keeping track of time, sequencing one thing after another, doing first things first

6 Rational
Drawing conclusions based on reason and fact

7 Digital
Using numbers, counting, calculating

8 Logical
Drawing conclusions based on logic, one thing following another in logical order, eg a mathematical theorem or a well-stated argument

9 Linear
Thinking in terms of linked ideas, one thought directly following another, often leading to a convergent conclusion

Right brain

A Concrete
Relating to things you can touch and feel

B Non-temporal
Without a sense of time

C Analogic
'Without logic', seeing likenesses between things, understanding metaphorical relationships

D Intuitive
Making leaps of insight, often based on incomplete patterns, hunches, feelings, or visual images

E Spatial
Seeing where things are in relation to other things and how parts go together to form a whole

F Synthetic
Putting things together to form wholes

G Non-verbal
Awareness of things, but minimal connection with words

H Holistic
Seeing things in their entirety, perceiving overall patterns and structures, often leading to divergent conclusions

I Non-rational
Not requiring a basis of reason or fact, willingness to suspend judgement

Answers   1 ___   2 ___   3 ___   4 ___   5 ___   6 ___   7 ___   8 ___   9 ___

Aim

This activity helps students identify their own learning preferences.

To the teacher

Make one copy of the worksheet and complete it yourself.

Which statements do you think refer more to the right brain and which to the left?

What do you learn about yourself as a learner? How is this reflected in your teaching style? Do you teach in a way which takes account of both sides of the brain?

Decide how to exploit this activity most effectively with your students.

Method

1 Make one copy of the worksheet for each student and hand them out. Students have these options. They can

- complete it themselves

- work in pairs and ask each other the questions, filling in the answers for their partner

- work in pairs and fill in the answers for their partner by guessing what he/she would write (using their knowledge of their partner)

2 Give students time to discuss their answers in pairs or small groups. If they have already done Activity 8, 'Left/Right Brain', ask them to identify the L/R brain preferences *before* you give the answers.

3 Read the Notes on the right to students to see if they recognise themselves. Did they notice any changes to their natural way of learning when they started school?

4 Ask students to identify teachers who they think are strongly right-brained or left-brained.

5 In groups, students suggest strategies they might use to maximise their own learning when they are with a teacher who does not share their learning preferences.

Level ✳ ✳

Notes

Do any of the following describe you when you were younger? Easily distracted, happy to entertain yourself, in danger of being a 'non-reader', you needed pictures to have reality present, got lost going to the classroom, used your fingers to count, daydreamed, had difficulty following directions, were good at sports, not so good at languages, a leader in class, chewed your tongue when working.

These behaviours are signs that you preferred right-brain learning.

Key

Students who have mainly 'a's tend to use their left brain more. Students with mainly 'b's tend to use their right brain more. You may also find that some students have an almost equal number of 'a's and 'b's, and/or that they have marked both answers for some of the choices. It is rare that anyone is completely right-brained or completely left-brained.

- Left-brain learners with a right-brain teacher will find it helpful to say the teacher's words silently in their heads during lessons to explain to themselves what the teacher is saying or doing; to study the coursebook after each lesson; to write or rewrite their notes logically and sequentially. They might also find it helpful to talk with a friend to clarify parts of the lesson not previously understood.

- Right-brain learners with a left-brain teacher will find it helpful to imagine acting out what they are hearing from the teacher, and to make lots of choices (any choices), eg *'Will I write this with a blue or black pen? Will I listen with both arms on the table or only one arm?'*; to produce diagrams or pictures as a form of note-taking to remember the content of the lesson, and when revising, to walk about and act out what is in their 'notes'.

✔ TICK the statement in each pair which is more true about you.

1 ____ a) I read the book, then view the movie.
  ____ b) I like to view the movie, then read the book.

2 ____ a) I experience life by reading about it.
  ____ b) I experience reality before reading about it.

3 ____ a) I analyse from the part to the whole.
  ____ b) I analyse from the whole to the part.

4 ____ a) I want information in written form.
  ____ b) I want information as a graph or chart or demonstration.

5 ____ a) I want to check work.
  ____ b) I find checking work is a nuisance.

6 ____ a) I need clear, specific, written instructions.
  ____ b) I love self-selected assignments that involve creativity.

7 ____ a) I have a tidy desk at home and at school.
  ____ b) I often have a messy desk at home and at school.

8 ____ a) I remember names, letters and/or numbers.
  ____ b) I remember places and events, but not names, letters or numbers.

9 ____ a) I am often quiet and still.
  ____ b) I am usually on the move.

10 ____ a) I like to complete work on time.
   ____ b) I have difficulty completing work on time.

11 ____ a) I like to see and hear people when relating to them.
   ____ b) I like to be near to and touch people when relating to them.

12 ____ a) I can explain why my answers are correct.
   ____ b) I give correct answers, but cannot explain why they are correct.

13 ____ a) I can recount events accurately in sequence.
   ____ b) I may exaggerate when re-telling an event.

14 ____ a) I accept the world as it is.
   ____ b) I try to change the world to meet my needs.

15 ____ a) I get above-average marks at school.
   ____ b) I often get average or below-average marks at school.

16 ____ a) I like to present tidy work and to be told exactly what work to do;
             I am less comfortable with lots of choices.
   ____ b) I make a mess of work which I am told to do; when I have
             a choice, the work is not a mess.

17 ____ a) I focus on what is happening inside myself.
   ____ b) I focus on what is happening outside myself.

18 ____ a) I prefer to leave things as they are.
   ____ b) I like to take things apart and put them back together again.

19 ____ a) I like to use words expressively.
   ____ b) I 'make faces' or use other forms of non-verbal communication.

20 ____ a) I talk in complete sentences.
   ____ b) I talk in phrases or I leave words out when talking.

Totals

a) _____

b) _____

Aim

This activity helps students understand the practical application of their own right/left brain preferences.

To the teacher

Make one copy of the worksheet and do the activity yourself.

Consider first which activities are related to which hemisphere – and the implications for your teaching. Then consider your own preferences – and whether you provide a balanced range of activites to take account of different learning preferences when you are teaching.

Decide how to exploit the activity most effectively with your students.

Method

1 Make one copy of the worksheet for each student.

2 Students work in pairs or small groups to decide which activities relate to which side of the brain, and then they decide individually which ones they are good at – checking their answers with a partner who knows them well, if they want to.

3 In small groups, students compare their answers and discuss the things they are good at.

4 Ask students to identify aspects of your teaching which appeal to the right and left sides of the brain. Can they suggest other things you can do?

5 Ask students if they know why you teach to the right brain, when language is located in the left brain. It is because the right brain learns 1600 times faster than the left!

Level ✳ ✳

Notes

In traditional language teaching, teachers predominantly used methods which were processed by the left hemisphere. The learners listened to the teacher and wrote down what the teacher said. They did a lot of reading and reciting, and language was taught as a set of facts and rules (vocabulary lists and grammar rules). In this kind of traditional language teaching, left-brain learners did well in examinations, but not necessarily as users of the language, while right-brain learners did much less well. Classes got more and more difficult to teach because the difference of level between the left-brain and right-brain learners got bigger and bigger.

To appeal to the right brain, language teachers incorporate music, drawing, movement, rhythm and choice. They teach connected sequences of language in context (eg realistic texts and dialogues) and give students the opportunity to use the language in ways which are meaningful for them.

Good language teachers use a combination of these two approaches.

Of course the left/right split is an oversimplification. If someone is relaxing and listening to music, they are predominantly using their right brain. When musicians are studying music, they are probably using their left brains. What particularly helps learning is the use of both sides of the brain at the same time (whole-brain learning) which creates links through the 'corpus callosum', the area which connects the two sides of the brain.

Incidentally, women's brains, on average, have many more links in the corpus callosum than men's!

Key

Left-hemisphere skills 1, 2, 4, 7, 10, 12, 15, 17, 18, 20

Right-hemisphere skills 3, 5, 6, 8, 9, 11, 13, 14, 16, 19

WRITE THE NUMBERS of the activities listed below in the hemisphere of the brain they are more strongly related to.

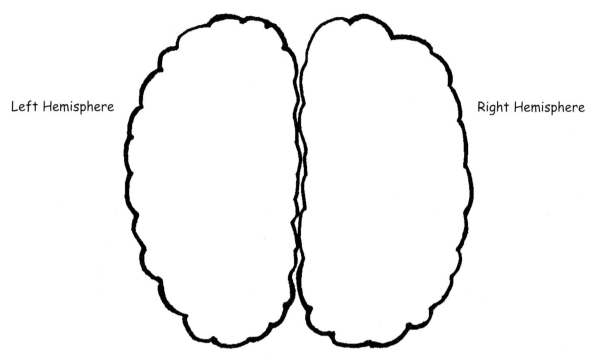

Left Hemisphere

Right Hemisphere

✔ TICK the activities you think you are particularly good at.

_____ 1   Reading

_____ 2   Listening

_____ 3   Singing and music

_____ 4   Language

_____ 5   Art expression (making or using pictures)

_____ 6   Feelings and emotions

_____ 7   Talking and reciting

_____ 8   Colour

_____ 9   Mathematical computation (adding, subtracting, multiplying, dividing)

_____ 10   Auditory association (eg you hear 'moo' and think 'cow')

_____ 11   Shapes and patterns

_____ 12   Following directions and rules

_____ 13   Spatial relationships

_____ 14   Creativity

_____ 15   Locating details and facts

_____ 16   Visualisation (picturing in your head)

_____ 17   Handwriting

_____ 18   Symbols (eg as used in maths and science)

_____ 19   Body awareness (knowing you are sitting or standing, etc)

_____ 20   Phonics (sounds in language which have meaning)

Aim

This free-standing activity can be done at any time to stimulate students to think and talk about their current priorities and preoccupations in life.

To the teacher

Before you read the Notes, read the worksheet and draw your own picture.

When you have finished, read the Notes and 'interpret' your picture. What do you think it shows about you? How accurate do you think it is?

Decide how to exploit the activity most effectively with your students.

Method

1   If you want to add anything to the worksheet, make one copy first, make your changes, and then make a copy for each student.

2   Before you hand out the copies, write the seven words on the board, check that the students know what they mean, and then brainstorm adjectives to describe the different items, writing them up as you go.

3   Give one copy of the worksheet to each student, read aloud the instructions, and give them time to draw.

4   In small groups, students show each other their pictures and talk about them.

5   Tell students the 'meanings', giving them time in their groups to talk after each meaning. They make notes about what their picture might mean.

6   Then, students look at the whole picture and the relationship between the parts (with practice of prepositions and comparatives!). What additional information does this give them?

7   In new groups, learners discuss, *'Is it true about me?'*

Extension

In the same groups (or in new groups), students discuss how they think their picture would have been different in the past (eg five years ago) and how it might change in the future (eg in five years' time).

Optional follow up

Students write about themselves, eg as an article in a newspaper, either now, in the past or in the future.

Level ✳

Notes

The *sun* and *cloud* are how you see life. Is the sun rising or sinking, is the cloud large or small, thick or thin, white or dark? Does the cloud cover the sun in any way?

The *house* is how you think about your home and family. Is it a big house, inhabited, simple, complex?

The *tree* is the big relationship in your life. Is it near the house or far away? Is it big or small, alive or dead, leafy or leafless?

The *path* is your path in life. Where does it start? Where does it end? Is it wide and straight? Is it curved? Does it change direction? Does it split?

The *bushes* are your friends. Are they near the house or far away? Are they big or small? Are they close together or far apart? How many groups of friends/bushes are there?

The *snake* is sex. What is it like? What is it associated with?

What is most important in your picture? Where are the things in relation to each other? Is the picture drawn quickly, or slowly and carefully? Is there a box around your picture or not? In which order did you draw the different things? Is your picture large or small? What does all this say about you?

Remember that this is a picture of you and the ways you are thinking today. If you drew the picture on another day, it might be very different.

PICTURE

Draw a picture which includes the seven items from the box below.

INTERPRETATION

sun _____

cloud _____

house _____

tree _____

snake _____

path _____

bushes _____

Aim

This activity introduces the concept of Visual, Auditory and Kinaesthetic (VAK) learning styles from Neuro-Linguistic Programming (NLP).

To the teacher

Make one copy of the worksheet and do the activity yourself. What are your strengths as a learner? What are your weaknesses?

Does your teaching reflect your strengths? Do you also take account of alternative learning preferences?

Decide how to exploit the activity most effectively with your students.

Method

1 Make one copy of the worksheet for each student.

2 Students complete the worksheet individually and add up their scores, although they might benefit from working together to make sure they understand all the sentences.

3 Read out the information in the Notes about 'VAKOG' and give students the answer key.

4 In small groups, students discuss their scores, similarities and differences. They decide what they can actually do to benefit from their strengths and compensate for their weaknesses.

Level ✳ ✳

Notes

According to the theories of Neuro-Linguistic Programming (NLP), developed by Richard Bandler and John Grinder, people take in information through their five senses, referred to as VAKOG: Visual, Auditory, Kinaesthetic, Olfactory and Gustatory. The three senses which people use primarily are V, A and K, and many people have a preference (strong or weak) for one or two of these.

It is helpful to know what our preferences are, so that we can take advantage of our natural learning style – and possibly learn to enhance the senses we don't use so readily.

Remember – most of us are quite capable of learning by using any of the senses. This analysis from NLP is simply about giving us the knowledge to help us learn more effectively – not about fitting people into limiting boxes. The more senses we use when taking in information, the easier it is to learn and remember that information.

People also process information using their senses internally too. Their sensory preferences for internal processing (thinking, imagining, remembering) might be different from their preferences for taking in information.

Ask students to add up their scores according to this table, which you can write on the board or ohp .

2	___	1	___	3	___
6	___	5	___	4	___
8	___	9	___	7	___
11	___	10	___	12	___
13	___	14	___	15	___
16	___	18	___	17	___
20	___	21	___	19	___
24	___	23	___	22	___
27	___	26	___	25	___
Total V	___	**A**	___	**K**	___

If you score 22 or more in one column, you have a strong preference for this way of learning. Make sure you use this sense when you are studying. Try developing the other senses too.

Key

V = preference for Visual learning

A = preference for Auditory learning

K = preference for Kinaesthetic learning

GRADE YOURSELF in each category, according to which statements seem most and least true of you. Give yourself 3 for the most true statement, 1 for the least true and 2 for the other one.

Learning

- [ ] 1 I learn by listening, by talking to others and by talking to myself in my head. I try out things by talking them through before doing them.
- [ ] 2 I learn by seeing. I need an overall view and purpose. I am cautious until I'm mentally clear. I like to see something first then do it.
- [ ] 3 I learn by doing, by manipulating things. I like 'hands on' experience. I do it first, then talk about it or see it being done.

Conversation

- [ ] 4 I'm not very talkative. I use gestures and movements. I use action words. I communicate feelings.
- [ ] 5 I'm talkative and may monopolise the conversation. I tell the whole of an event in sequence.
- [ ] 6 I need the whole picture and lots of detail. I select carefully what to say. I communicate vision and pictures.

Reading

- [ ] 7 I enjoy action-packed books and stories with a strong plot. I reflect the story with body movements and feelings while reading. I point while reading.
- [ ] 8 I'm a strong, successful, fast, quiet reader. I prefer to read than be read to.
- [ ] 9 I enjoy reading aloud and listening. I'm confident with unknown words. I can be slow because I'm saying words in my head.

Self

- [ ] 10 I'm easily distracted. I can repeat things accurately. I can mimic accents, tone, pitch and timbre, eg other people's voices. I speak rhythmically.
- [ ] 11 I'm neat, orderly, quiet, observant and organised. Appearance is important.
- [ ] 12 I move a lot. I respond to physical rewards, eg touching rather than words. I touch people and stand close to them.

Remembering

- [ ] 13 I remember what I see. I memorise by picturing. I have problems remembering verbal instructions.
- [ ] 14 I remember words or what I hear. I memorise by repeating words in my head.
- [ ] 15 I remember an overall impression of what I experience. I memorise by doing.

Writing

- [ ] 16 I have naturally neat handwriting. I like my writing to look good. I'm quiet, careful and deliberate.
- [ ] 17 My writing is thick, pressured and unclear. I'm a physical, emotional writer.
- [ ] 18 I'm better at talking than writing. I like to talk to others or myself while writing.

Spelling

- [ ] 19 I count out letters with body movements, eg moving my finger. I check my spelling with my internal feelings.
- [ ] 20 I'm an accurate speller. I see the words. I'm confused about spelling words I've never seen before.
- [ ] 21 I spell words as they sound (phonetically) not as they look. I spell rhythmically.

Imagination

- [ ] 22 I want to walk while imagining. I like to act out the image. I'm weak on details, strong on actions and emotions.
- [ ] 23 I hear sounds and voices. I'm good at sequences and creating dialogue. I'm responsive to music.
- [ ] 24 I see vivid images. I can see possibilities, details appear. I'm good at long-term planning and on overviews.

Voice

- [ ] 25 When speaking, my chin is down, my voice is loud.
- [ ] 26 I use different tones and melody.
- [ ] 27 When speaking, my chin is up, my voice is high. I speak fast.

Aim

This activity helps students become aware of the value of various language learning activities. It is helpful if they are already aware of their own learning preferences (possibly after completing 'Learning Preferences', Activity 12).

To the teacher

Make one copy of the worksheet and do the activity yourself. Then tick the number of any activity you have done in class in the last four weeks. Put a tick for each time you have done an activity.

Do you notice anything about the balance of your teaching activities? Are there any activities you could be doing more of? Is there any particular type of student who is likely to be doing less well because of your teaching preferences? Does this correspond to specific individuals in your classes – particularly those who might not be succeeding? Choose three of the activities to do in class in the next week.

Decide how to exploit the activity most effectively with your students.

Method

1   Make one copy of the worksheet for each student.

2   Students work together in small groups to complete the worksheet.

3   Students form new groups containing someone from each of the previous groups. They compare their answers. (Note that many of the activities are multi-sensory and that the suggested answers relate only to the primary sense.)

4   They work individually and circle the ten activities they enjoy most.

5   Tell students that they are going to work in groups of five and each person is going to try to 'sell' their three favourite learning activities to the others. By the end of the selling period, each person should have chosen five activities in addition to the ones already circled on their sheet.

6   Students now work individually and use a different colour to circle the ten activities they *least* enjoy.

7   Ask them to compare their various choices with what they know of their preferred learning style. Probably the first activities they chose are the ones which most favour their preferred style – they should do these when they want to feel motivated or safe while studying. The ones they least like are probably the ones which least favour their preferred learning style – they should do these when they are ready to be challenged to extend their learning abilities.

Level   ✳ ✳

Key

V   1, 4, 5, 11, 13, 15, 17, 18, 29, 31, 34, 37, 40, 41, 44, 46, 47, 52, 54, 56

A   2, 7, 10, 14, 16, 20, 21, 23, 25, 27, 28, 35, 36, 39, 43, 45, 49

K   3, 6, 8, 9, 12, 19, 22, 24, 26, 30, 32, 33, 38, 42, 48, 50, 51, 53, 55

DECIDE which strategies will help you learn visually (V), auditorily (A) or kinaesthetically (K).

To motivate you to SPEAK

___ 1 Create a story from pictures.

___ 2 Connect sounds to a story.

___ 3 Do roleplay.

___ 4 See a TV documentary and discuss.

___ 5 Create a story from lists of words.

___ 6 Speak with emotions and gestures.

___ 7 Create a radio programme.

___ 8 Do group work.

___ 9 Do drama and simulations.

___ 10 Listen to the radio or a tape, and discuss.

___ 11 Watch a video and discuss.

___ 12 Do activities involving actions, eg going in and out of the room.

___ 13 Look at art, and discuss.

___ 14 Ask someone to give clear instructions and to ask questions to help discussion.

To motivate you to WRITE

___ 27 Talk in pairs, then write about it.

___ 28 Write roleplays and sketches.

___ 29 Draw and write comic strips.

___ 30 One person mimes/gestures, the others write down what they understand.

___ 31 Fill in blanks in texts.

___ 32 Create written dramas.

___ 33 Apply for jobs and be interviewed.

___ 34 Read adverts and answer them.

___ 35 Listen to dictations; fill in gaps in a text.

___ 36 Listen to tapes, then summarise.

___ 37 Use several pictures to make a story.

___ 38 Create a class newspaper.

___ 39 Write dialogues.

___ 40 Picture a situation, then write about it.

___ 41 Write on picture postcards.

___ 42 Write problem-page letters.

___ 43 Dictate to each other in pairs.

To motivate you to LISTEN

___ 15 Have pictures of new words.

___ 16 Watch videos without sound, then listen to the soundtrack.

___ 17 Make mental pictures of what you are going to listen to or have heard.

___ 18 Listen while you're watching pictures.

___ 19 Pause the video or tape and act the scene, then continue to listen.

___ 20 Give talks or tell stories.

___ 21 Read the book while listening to the tape.

___ 22 Listen, then continue the story.

___ 23 Different people listen to different parts of a story, then share.

___ 24 Gesture, mimic or move while listening.

___ 25 Cover the video screen and listen.

___ 26 Listen to instructions and do the actions, eg make a paper plane.

To motivate you to READ

___ 44 Discuss the book cover.

___ 45 Read aloud.

___ 46 Describe the pictures in the book.

___ 47 See the video or photos, then read.

___ 48 Make gestures and actions as you read.

___ 49 Record yourself reading.

___ 50 Imagine you are in the text.

___ 51 Act out the story.

___ 52 Create a poster of what you read.

___ 53 Put a cut-up text in the correct order, then read it.

___ 54 Describe settings for what you read.

___ 55 Read aloud with actions and gestures.

___ 56 Draw pictures to illustrate the story.

Aim

This activity helps students understand their learning preferences and enhance their visual learning techniques.

To the teacher

Make one copy of the worksheet and do the activity yourself *as a student*. What do you learn about your preferred study habits? How is this reflected in your preferred teaching style? Do you include a balance of activities for students whose preferences are different from your own? Note any activities you haven't done recently in class and plan to incorporate them into lessons soon.

Decide how to exploit the activity most effectively with your students.

Method

1 Make one copy of the worksheet for each student and hand them out.

2 In pairs, students work through the questions indicating which techniques they usually use. They ask each other the statements as questions and fill in their partner's answers.

3 In pairs or small groups, students compare their techniques and decide what sort of techniques (in what sort of sequence) they are using – visual, auditory or kinaesthetic?

4 Compare students' understanding of the techniques they are using with the suggested answers below.

5 Ask students to identify the most effective study methods – and encourage them to try different approaches (with appropriate language learning activities) in subsequent lessons.

Suggested answers

Learners may be thinking in the following ways:

1 A to K to V. You are trying to see what you hear.
2 V to K to V. You are trying to picture what you read.
3 V to V. You are good at making pictures in your head.
4 A to V. You are good at making pictures in your head.
5 Mainly V. You are wanting to see the notes.
6 Mainly K. You are wanting to make the notes, not see them.
7 K and V, mainly V. You are wanting to see the notes re-done neatly.
8 K. It is the action of making notes that helps you.
9 Very V. You don't need any K involvement (eg writing).
10 V. You are adding colour to aid memory.
11 V, A and K, right brain and left brain.
12 A first. If the teacher isn't there, talk to a friend.
13 V first. Read the coursebook before the lesson.
14 K and V. You are wanting an overview.
15 Lists are more A (left brain).
16 Diagrams are more V and K (right brain).

Level ✳ ✳ ✳

Notes

Visual learners, and those who process and remember information visually, are those who learn most quickly and efficiently. They are also the learners favoured by most school systems in the west.

In tests, people who use visual techniques see the questions and very quickly scan their memory for the answers. The answers to different questions may be stored in quite different places, but the visual scan finds them very quickly.

People who use auditory techniques see the questions and 'insert the audio cassette' in their memory, starting at the beginning, listening to the inner voice. When they hear the information they need, they write it down. Valuable time is taken up 'playing through the tape' in the brain. It's best to transfer from auditory to visual memory before a test.

Lots of kinaesthetic people see the questions in a test and access feelings, emotions and bodily movements associated with the answers. Their fingers or bodies dance. Sometimes the answer takes a long time to come. Sometimes it is instantaneous. It's more efficient to transfer from kinaesthetic to visual memory before a test.

Students can practise using the most effective (visual) strategies (see ★ below), and you can explain to students what you are doing and why, and enhance their visual learning strategies by doing the following:

• Write on paper or OHTs rather than on boards. Keep the paper or OHTs to show several times in future weeks (or display them on the wall).

• If you use mindmaps, encourage students to make their own. If they copy yours, they can colour them themselves and add their own words and drawings.

• Write words high on the board. Encourage learners to keep their heads up and 'look up inside their heads' to find words, pictures and ideas.

• Encourage learners to take 'mental snapshots' of words, whole sentences or even whole posters – and then close their eyes and try to see them again. (Keep repeating the process until they can 'see' the item in their mind's eye.)

★ The most effective (visual) study techniques are: 3, 4, 5, 7, 9, 10, 11, 13, 14, 16

HOW DO YOU STUDY? Read the statements and circle 'Yes' or 'No'. Write a sentence about how each technique helps you learn. Choose the 10 study techniques you think are most effective.

Yes / No 1   I write notes in talks to help me picture/remember what I am learning.

Yes / No 2   I write notes to help me picture/remember what I am reading.

Yes / No 3   When I read, I picture in my head what I am reading.

Yes / No 4   When I am listening to a talk, I picture in my head what I am hearing.

Yes / No 5   When I make notes, I read them afterwards.

Yes / No 6   When I make notes, I never look at them afterwards.

Yes / No 7   When I make notes, I re-write them afterwards.

Yes / No 8   I need to experience the action of writing when I am listening.

Yes / No 9   I prefer to take notes, rather than to receive a typed handout.

Yes / No 10 When I revise, I highlight my notes using different colours.

Yes / No 11 I make spider diagrams or mindmaps when taking notes or when revising.

Yes / No 12 I prefer to listen to the teacher before I read the coursebook.

Yes / No 13 I prefer to read the coursebook before I listen to the teacher.

Yes / No 14 I like to condense all the information on a topic onto one page or into one diagram.

Yes / No 15 I prefer lists to diagrams.

Yes / No 16 I prefer diagrams to lists.

Aim

This activity helps students make the most of learning opportunities with different teachers. It assumes that students have already identified their own preferred VAK learning styles.

To the teacher

Make a copy of the worksheet and tick which statements are true about you as a teacher. It is useful to know your preferred teaching style so that you can cater for more of your students by consciously using techniques which come less naturally to you.

Think about students who are doing less well in your classes and decide what you think their learning styles might be (you can compare your guesses with their evaluation when they have completed the activity). Plan ways to teach more effectively students with whom you have less rapport.

Decide how to exploit this activity most effectively with your students.

Method

1 Make one copy of the worksheet for each student and hand them out.

2 Students work in groups to analyse your style as a teacher and report back to the whole class. Do you agree with them? Compare their assessment of you with your assessment of yourself.

   If you receive negative feedback (whether deserved or not), your relationship with your students will almost certainly improve if you accept it with good humour (outwardly, at least!).

3 Students work in small groups and discuss teachers they know or have known. Emphasise that they are considering teaching styles and not just taking an opportunity to criticise teachers. (You might also say that it would be unprofessional for you to hear negative feedback about colleagues.)

4 Still in their groups, students think about their own learning preferences in relation to the different teachers. Which teachers teach in the way they most like to learn? Is there a relationship between people they have thought of as 'good' teachers and those teachers who share their learning style?

5 In their groups, students write advice to others to help them take advantage of different teaching styles.

Level ✳ ✳ ✳

Key

Visual Learner – Visual Teacher
Looks good! You're OK. This teacher learns like you and probably thinks you are a good learner and you probably think he/she is a good teacher.

Auditory Learner – Visual Teacher
Talk to yourself in your head to put into words what the teacher is showing you. At home read parts of the coursebook aloud. Talk to a friend about the lessons. Talk on the phone about homework. Write questions to ask the teacher. Show your teacher your questions. Talk about any drawing, picture or diagram.

Kinaesthetic Learner – Visual Teacher
Imagine yourself to be in the pictures and moving through the diagrams. Choose favourite words and ask yourself how you feel in the lessons and about the topics. Draw an action picture or active diagram for how you feel in each lesson. At home, act out the new words and grammar of each lesson.

Visual Learner – Auditory Teacher
Picture what the teacher is saying. Do drawings or diagrams of what the teacher has said. Copy drawings or diagrams from the coursebook or library books on topics you can't picture clearly.

Auditory Learner – Auditory Teacher
Sounds good! You're OK. This teacher learns like you and probably thinks you are a good learner and you probably think he/she is a good teacher.

Kinaesthetic Learner – Auditory Teacher
Watch the teacher's face as he/she talks. Try to guess the feelings of the teacher about the topic and words in the lesson. Imagine acting out the meanings of new words and grammar. Imagine the teacher is talking about you and your life. At home, move around 'being' the new words, new grammar and topics.

Visual Learner – Kinaesthetic Teacher
Ask the teacher if you can sometimes observe rather than join in the activities. Picture what the teacher is doing and saying. Look in the coursebook to see what the teacher is doing.

Auditory Learner – Kinaesthetic Teacher
Talk to yourself in your head to put into words what the teacher is doing and getting you to do. Ask for time to take notes after an activity. At home, read parts of the coursebook aloud. Ask other learners questions. Ask the teacher if you and a partner can observe and talk during some activities.

Kinaesthetic Learner – Kinaesthetic Teacher
Feels good! You're OK. This teacher learns like you and probably thinks you are a good learner and you probably think he/she is a good teacher.

WHICH DESCRIPTIONS apply to which of your teachers (present and/or past)?

VISUAL	AUDITORY	KINAESTHETIC
talks fast	speaks rhythmically	talks more slowly
uses visual aids, pictures, drawings, diagrams	uses class discussion, question and answer	uses things to touch, eg handouts and objects
likes to cover a lot eg lots of words, materials,	gets students to read aloud, likes chorus drills	likes students to be active, eg roleplay, action games
thinks form is important, eg grammar, spelling; work must look good	thinks talking is important, says 'OK, right', repeats what students say	thinks concepts and ideas are more important than grammar and spelling
believes in visual feedback eg written tests	believes in spoken feedback eg 'Why don't you …'	believes in active feedback eg what learners can do
likes work done 'at the right time, on the right day'	likes students to ask questions so he/she can speak	likes groupwork, teamwork and students writing on the board
likes beautiful posters and coloured pens	talks a lot, comments when learners are speaking, 'Mm, ah'	uses lots of actions, gestures, and demonstrations

Teachers:

_____   _____   _____

_____   _____   _____

WHAT ADVICE would you give students when they are in class with teachers whose teaching style does not match their learning style?

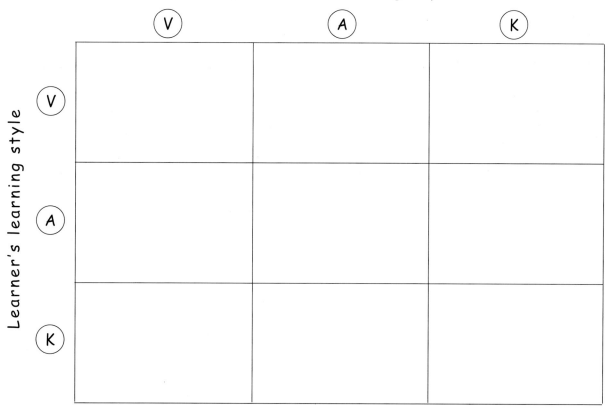

Teacher's teaching style

Aim

As well as being a fascinating language exercise, this activity explores how we use our 'inner senses' when we remember or imagine things.

To the teacher

Make two copies of the worksheet and do the activity yourself with a friend.

Notice how you think in different ways from your partner. Notice too what you find easy and less easy about this activity.

Decide how to exploit the activity most effectively with your students.

Method

1   Give a copy of the worksheet to each student.

2   Students work in pairs. First, As ask questions of Bs and note their eye movements. Bs think of their answers, but do not say anything.

   Then As ask Bs the questions again. Bs say the answers to the questions this time and say what they were thinking. As tell them how their eyes moved.

3   Students exchange roles and Bs ask As the second set of questions.

4   Discuss with students the information on this page about how people's eye movements can show how they are thinking. You might stimulate students' interest with the question, *'How can you tell when people are lying?'* The answer is, of course, that their eye movements will often give them away. If they are inventing information (rather than remembering the truth), they will probably look up and to their right!

   When students are doing this activity, they may find it difficult to act naturally. View this as an opportunity to practise watching eye movements. The real fun begins when you walk out of the classroom and watch people's eye movements when they don't know they're being watched!

   The trick is to notice the sequence of movements, and the last place the person looks is where they 'found' the image they were looking for. Even if someone tries to answer the questions without moving their eyes, once they think you have stopped watching, they almost always quickly look to where their image is stored, just to check (maybe unconsciously) that it really is there.

Key

Questions 1, 4, 5 are visual.

Questions 2, 6, 8 are auditory.

Questions 3, 7, 9 are kinaesthetic.

Question 10 depends on how each individual is thinking.

Level   ✳ ✳

Eye movements

When people are remembering or imagining, they tend to use three different types of thinking, in various sequences:

Visual – thinking in pictures and images

Auditory – thinking in words, voices or sounds

Kinaesthetic – thinking in actions, movements and feelings

When people are thinking, they tend literally to look at the place where their thought is situated in their heads, so you can tell from their eyes how (not what) they are thinking.

For example, if you ask me, *'What does it feel like to touch a zebra?'*, I have never touched a zebra, so I might look up to my left to remember seeing a zebra, then up left again to remember a horse. Then I might look down right to remember touching a horse, then up left to remember seeing the zebra, and then down right again to imagine touching the zebra.

Some people, when they remember visually, look straight ahead, with their eyes unfocused. Not everyone follows the 'usual' pattern: they will have their own pattern and they will stick to it.

If students think they have difficulty seeing internal pictures, they might find it easier if they look up!

You are looking at the eye of the person.

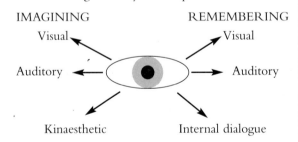

IMAGINING   REMEMBERING

Visual   Visual

Auditory   Auditory

Kinaesthetic   Internal dialogue

The general pattern for eye movements is:

Visualising – up

Listening – to the side

Feeling – down right (their right)

Remembering – left (their left)

Imagining (creating) – right

Internal dialogue (talking to yourself) – down left

Eye movements were described by Richard Bandler and John Grinder, the founders of NLP (Neuro-Linguistic Programming), in their book *Frogs Into Princes*, Real People Press 1979.

STAGE ONE Sit where you can see your partner's eyes but not facing him/her. Your partner doesn't look directly at you. Ask the questions. As your partner thinks about the answers, watch and draw the sequence of his/her eye movements.

STAGE TWO Ask the questions again. This time your partner answers the questions and says what he/she was thinking. Write down what he/she says and say how his/her eyes moved.

Questions for A to ask B	Eye movements	Answer/Comment
1 What's your favourite colour?	○○ ○○ ○○ ○○	_____
2 What's your favourite music group?	○○ ○○ ○○ ○○	_____
3 What's your favourite sport to play?	○○ ○○ ○○ ○○	_____
4 How would you look with green ears?	○○ ○○ ○○ ○○	_____
5 Can you picture a beautiful sunset?	○○ ○○ ○○ ○○	_____
6 Can you hear some beautiful music?	○○ ○○ ○○ ○○	_____
7 Can you feel yourself swimming?	○○ ○○ ○○ ○○	_____
8 What is the worst noise?	○○ ○○ ○○ ○○	_____
9 When do you feel very good?	○○ ○○ ○○ ○○	_____
10 How does it feel to be relaxed?	○○ ○○ ○○ ○○	_____

Questions for B to ask A	Eye movements	Answer/Comment
1 What colour is your front door?	○○ ○○ ○○ ○○	_____
2 What's your favourite song?	○○ ○○ ○○ ○○	_____
3 What's your favourite weather?	○○ ○○ ○○ ○○	_____
4 How would you look with blue hair?	○○ ○○ ○○ ○○	_____
5 Can you picture a mountain?	○○ ○○ ○○ ○○	_____
6 Can your hear birds singing?	○○ ○○ ○○ ○○	_____
7 How does it feel to take a shower?	○○ ○○ ○○ ○○	_____
8 What is the most beautiful sound?	○○ ○○ ○○ ○○	_____
9 When do you feel happiest?	○○ ○○ ○○ ○○	_____
10 How does it feel to be asleep?	○○ ○○ ○○ ○○	_____

Aim

This free-standing activity can be approached as entertaining language practice, but it also helps students think about their approach to important issues, such as life, death and problems, etc.

To the teacher

Before you read the Notes, make one copy of the worksheet, sit quietly and answer the questions in relation to yourself.

When you have finished, read the Notes and interpret your answer. What do you learn about yourself? Is it accurate?

Decide how to exploit the activity most effectively with your students.

Method

1   Give one copy of the worksheet to each student. Play some relaxing music. Read each sentence aloud and give students time to listen, think and write, before moving on to the next one.

Alternatively:

Don't give out the worksheet yet. Tell the students they are going to do a guided relaxation. Students sit quietly and follow your voice with their eyes closed, as you read out the sentences on the worksheet, pausing between each one. When they have thought about all the sentences in this way, you can hand out the worksheet for them to complete it individually.

2   In small groups, students discuss what they have written.

3   Tell students the interpretations of the different aspects of the journey, giving them time to talk in their groups after each 'meaning'.

4   In new small groups, students discuss, *'Do I think this is true about me?'*

Optional follow up

Students write about themselves, eg their ideal obituary in a newspaper.

Level   ✳

Notes

The forest is how you see life.

The path is your path through life. What is the path like? Do you follow it?

The bear is how you see problems in your life. What is the bear like?

How you get past the bear is how you deal with problems.

The house is the supernatural (or religion, or God). What is the house like?

What you do to the house is how you behave in relation to religion, God or the supernatural.

The river is sex, your attitude to sex.

How you get across the river is how you behave in relation to sex.

The wall is death.

How you get to the other side of the wall is how you deal with death.

The other side of the wall is what you believe there is after death.

Imagine the following situations.

You are in a FOREST. Describe what you can see, hear and feel.

_____

You see a PATH. Describe the path and say if you follow the path or not.

_____

You see a BEAR. Describe the bear.

_____

Describe how you get past the bear.

_____

You see a HOUSE. Describe the house.

_____

Do you go inside the house? Do you walk around the outside of the house?
Describe what you do and what you see, hear and feel.

_____

You see a RIVER. Describe the river.

_____

Describe how you cross the river.

_____

You see a WALL. Describe the wall.

_____

Describe how you get to the other side of the wall.

_____

Describe what is on the other side of the wall.

_____

Aim

This activity introduces the concept of Multiple Intelligences and helps students identify the ways in which they are intelligent.

To the teacher

Make a copy of the worksheet and complete it for yourself. What do you learn about your strengths and preferences?

Can you see ways in which your strengths and preferences are reflected in your teaching? Do you take account of students whose strengths and preferences are different from yours?

Decide how to exploit the activity most effectively with your students.

Method

1 Make a copy of the worksheet for each student. Students work in pairs, and using what they know of the other person, without speaking, they fill in the first section of the worksheet for their partner by guessing what the other person would write for themselves.

2 Individuals then read what their partner has written, and form small groups to discuss ways in which their partner was right or wrong – or possibly how their partner knows some things about them that they didn't know about themselves.

3 In their groups, students complete the second part of the worksheet.

4 Discuss as a class the names they invent for the different intelligences and then read them the information about Howard Gardner's Multiple Intelligences (see Notes).

5 Ask students to consider which school subjects (English, other languages, mathematics, physics, chemistry, biology, history, geography, art, craft, sports, etc) most correspond to each type of intelligence. Can they see a link between the subjects they are/were good at and the intelligences they have identified for themselves?

Optional follow up

In their groups, students identify the sorts of jobs which would suit people who excel in the different intelligences. Students act out careers interviews. The 'careers adviser' asks questions to find out what sorts of things the interviewee is good at and then suggests possible jobs. The interviewees can either answer questions truthfully about themselves, or they can imagine someone in a particular job and answer questions from their point of view to see if the careers adviser suggests that job.

Level ✳ ✳

Notes

Howard Gardner has identified different kinds of intelligence, other than the traditionally recognised 'linguistic' and 'logical-mathematical'. He originally identified seven intelligences, then added the eighth, 'naturalist'. His names for the intelligences are:

1 **Linguistic** Using words and language, speaking, reading, writing (journalist, writer, public speaker)

2 **Logical-Mathematical** Reasoning, using logic, problem-solving, manipulating numbers (scientist, mathematician, accountant)

3 **Spatial-Visual** Visualising, appreciating art (in three dimensions), having a sense of direction (artist, sculptor, navigator)

4 **Bodily-Kinaesthetic** Having physical, body skills, prowess and awareness (dancer, keep-fit trainer, athlete)

5 **Musical** Composing, performing, appreciating, recognising music (composer, musician, singer, conductor)

6 **Interpersonal** Good team member, organising and leading groups, resolving conflicts (sales person, counsellor, teacher)

7 **Intrapersonal** Self-knowledge, introspection, awareness and control of self (philosopher, religious devotee)

8 **Naturalist** Analysing similarities and differences, categorising, an interest in animals, plants, weather and the environment (vet, botanist, astronomer)

Very few people are only skilled in one area of intelligence. Most of us have aspects of many different intelligences which we use in many different ways in our lives – our jobs, our personal relationships, our hobbies, etc. The aim of considering different intelligences is to recognise more options for us all and help us make the most of our potential. It is not to limit people's potential by putting them into boxes.

Daniel Goleman has also referred to 'Emotional Intelligence' (in his book of that name), which overlaps with Gardner's Intrapersonal and Interpersonal Intelligences, and Danah Zohar has suggested a 'Spiritual Intelligence', which might be related to Intrapersonal Intelligence.

✔ TICK the boxes to show what you love, what you need, and how you think.

	I LOVE	I NEED	I THINK
1	☐ word games, reading, writing, telling stories	☐ books, tapes, pens, pencils, paper, dialogue	☐ in words, discussion, debate, stories
2	☐ puzzles, experimenting, questioning, calculating	☐ exploration and discovery, science materials	☐ by reasoning
3	☐ designing, drawing, doodling, picturing things in my head	☐ art, video, movies, pictures, puzzles, imagination games	☐ in images and pictures
4	☐ dancing, running, jumping, building, touching, gesturing	☐ sports, physical games, drama, movement, touching	☐ through my body's feelings
5	☐ singing, whistling, humming, tapping rhythms	☐ music, at home and school, musical instruments	☐ through rhythm and melody
6	☐ leading, organising, partying, relating to others, getting other people to do things	☐ teaching people, community events, being taught, clubs, friends, group games	☐ by interacting with other people
7	☐ being quiet, planning, writing a diary, dreaming, meditating, setting goals	☐ secret places, time alone, projects I choose myself, to do in my own way	☐ deeply inside myself
8	☐ nature, collecting, sorting things into categories	☐ to observe and classify things, the natural world	☐ by comparing things

Each number represents a different kind of intelligence. Create a name for each of the intelligences.

1 ▭   5 ▭

2 ▭   6 ▭

3 ▭   7 ▭

4 ▭   8 ▭

WRITE the numbers in the order which most describes you.

Most me ◄ —————————— ► Least me

☐ ☐ ☐ ☐ ☐ ☐ ☐ ☐

Aim

This activity focuses on how the language people use can give an insight into their preferred ways of thinking. It is designed to follow on from 'Multiple Intelligences', Activity 18.

To the teacher

Make a copy of the worksheet and complete it for yourself.

Can you think of other examples of language which might reflect the different intelligences?

Decide how to exploit the activity most effectively with your students.

Method

1   Make a copy of the worksheet for each student.

2   Students work in small groups to sort the language under the different headings.

3   Check the answers with the whole class. You might make the activity a competition, with groups earning points for getting the correct answer – and also for challenging an answer and making a reasonable case for suggesting that the language might reflect a different intelligence.

4   In their groups, students make up other examples of 'intelligence-specific' language. Other groups guess which intelligence is being referred to.

Level ✷ ✷

Key	
Linguistic	1, 13, 23, 30, 33
Logical–Mathematical	2, 12, 21, 32, 40
Spatial–Visual	7, 14, 22, 24, 31, 34
Bodily–Kinaesthetic	3, 8, 20, 25, 36
Musical	5, 9, 18, 27, 37
Interpersonal	6, 10, 16, 28, 38
Intrapersonal	4, 15, 17, 29, 39
Naturalist	11, 19, 26, 35

The language people use can often express their preferred ways of thinking and working. Sort the following language according to the eight different intelligences identified by Howard Gardner.

Howard Gardner's Multiple Intelligences

Linguistic	☐	☐	☐	☐	☐	☐
Logical-Mathematical	☐	☐	☐	☐	☐	☐
Spatial-Visual	☐	☐	☐	☐	☐	☐
Bodily-Kinaesthetic	☐	☐	☐	☐	☐	☐
Musical	☐	☐	☐	☐	☐	☐
Interpersonal	☐	☐	☐	☐	☐	☐
Intrapersonal	☐	☐	☐	☐	☐	☐
Naturalist	☐	☐	☐	☐	☐	☐

1 Can you put that into words?

2 What are the figures?

3 I know how you feel.

4 I need to think about that.

5 That's just like the song/the music …

6 *I* think this, what do *you* think?

7 Look at it this way.

8 What does it feel like?

9 I could sing that idea.

10 Let's discuss it.

11 I really enjoyed walking through the park to get here.

12 Do you have the statistics?

13 Tell me all about it.

14 I can't quite see how it all fits together.

15 I can't think with all these things going on.

16 Tell me, I'll soon say if I agree or not.

17 I wrote a poem about you in my diary.

18 What a beautiful voice.

19 Can we sort these things into separate groups?

20 Let me show you what it does.

21 How do you calculate that?

22 It was a very colourful experience.

23 It's very interesting how you said that.

24 I need to picture it.

25 Watch me, it happened like this …

26 So which bits are the same and which are different?

27 Can you hear the birds/insects/wind/water?

28 Let's do it together.

29 It may seem unimportant to you, but I'll have to think it through by myself.

30 I have lots of favourite words.

31 Yes, but what does it/he/she look like?

32 That's not logical.

33 I love languages.

34 Show me a picture.

35 Let's get outside under the stars.

36 I need to do it to understand.

37 'La-la-la.' I'm just singing to myself.

38 Let's get together with other people to do it.

39 I'd rather do it my way.

40 What's the rule here?

Aim

This activity helps students understand that they are in possession of a range of skills and capabilities.

To the teacher

Make a copy of the questionnaire and do it yourself.

What do you learn about yourself? How does this relate to your teaching? Do you take account of your own intelligences as well as the differing intelligences of others?

Decide how to exploit the activity most effectively with your students.

Method

1   Make a copy of the worksheet for each student.

2   Students complete their questionnaire individually, although they could work in pairs (with a dictionary), as an aid to comprehension. At lower language levels, read each sentence aloud and make sure they understand the meaning before they answer.

3   When they reach the end, students discuss which numbers refer to which intelligences and then score their own questionnaires against the key, which you could photocopy or write on the board.

4   Ask students the following questions, which they discuss in small groups. (All these questions are in the present tense, but you can change it to the past tense depending on the age/stage of your students.)

•   *What does it mean if you have put a lot of ticks across a range of intelligences? What does it mean if you have only put a few ticks? If all your ticks are in the same intelligence?*

•   *Which intelligences do you naturally use a lot? Which ones do you not use very often?*

•   *Which subject are you good at in school? Which ones do you not get good grades in? Which ones do you like or dislike?*

•   *Can you see any link between the intelligences you use the most and the subjects you like most or get best grades in? Is there a link between the intelligences you use less and the subjects in which you do not do so well?*

•   *Think about your teachers for the different subjects. Do they teach you in ways which make it easier for you to learn? Can you find any link between the different intelligences and the ways they teach? Can you see any link between the ways they teach and the intelligences you use more or less?*

5   Students consider each person in the group in turn and help them decide on ways they can maximise their strengths. How can they use their intelligences to do better at subjects or to learn from teachers who they do not learn from naturally?

6   Ask students to work in small groups to identify the intelligences they think *you* use as a teacher. Share their ideas with the whole class. They then form new small groups and suggest things you could do as a teacher which might help them individually to learn more effectively.

Level   ✳ ✳

Notes

People usually tick boxes across a range of intelligences, although certain broad trends might emerge. This activity is not about labelling and limiting students, it is about helping them understand their range of skills, capabilities and intelligences – and the fact that everyone is different and intelligent in different ways. Once we are aware of our strengths and weaknesses, we are more able to operate most effectively.

Students who put a lot of ticks across a range of intelligences are probably good all-rounders. Those who put most of their ticks in one intelligence may well be very gifted in that particular area.

Key
Multiple Intelligences Profile

Type of Intelligence	Question numbers
Linguistic	1, 7, 11, 31, 35
Logical-Mathematical	10, 24, 30, 33, 38
Spatial-Visual	8, 15, 18, 20, 36
Musical	2, 16, 21, 28, 34
Bodily-Kinaesthetic	3, 14, 25, 29, 40
Interpersonal	5, 13, 17, 22, 37
Intrapersonal	6, 9, 19, 23, 27
Naturalist	4, 12, 26, 32, 39

✔ Most of us have a mixture of different intelligences – the interesting thing is to find out each person's unique profile. What is yours? Put a tick against each item that is true about you.

____ 1 I can hear words in my head before I speak or write them down.

____ 2 I often have music playing while I'm studying or working.

____ 3 I play at least one sport or physical activity regularly.

____ 4 I enjoy being out in the countryside and feel 'trapped' in cities.

____ 5 I prefer group sports to solo sports.

____ 6 I keep a personal diary or journal.

____ 7 I learn more from listening or reading than I do from TV or films.

____ 8 I often see clear visual images when I close my eyes.

____ 9 I regularly spend time alone meditating, or thinking about important questions.

____ 10 I like things to be measured, analysed, categorised or quantified in some way.

____ 11 English and history are easier for me than maths and science.

____ 12 I am very interested in ecology and preserving the planet.

____ 13 People come to me for advice.

____ 14 My best ideas often come to me when I'm walking or doing something physical.

____ 15 I can generally find my way around unfamiliar territory.

____ 16 I often make tapping sounds or sing melodies while working or studying.

____ 17 I enjoy teaching people what I know.

____ 18 I find it much easier to do geometry than algebra.

____ 19 I consider myself to be strong-willed or fiercely independent.

____ 20 I can easily imagine how something would look from all angles.

____ 21 If I hear a tune once or twice, I can usually sing it fairly accurately, and I can tell if a note is out of tune.

____ 22 I consider myself (or others have called me) a leader.

____ 23 I read books or attend seminars to learn more about myself.

____ 24 I believe that most things have a rational explanation.

____ 25 I find it difficult to sit still for long.

____ 26 I like classifying things and sorting them into categories.

____ 27 I have a special hobby or interest that I mostly keep to myself.

____ 28 I play an instrument and/or I know the tunes to many songs or pieces of music.

____ 29 I need to practise a new skill by doing it rather hearing about it or seeing it.

____ 30 I wonder about how things work.

____ 31 I enjoy word games, tongue twisters, nonsense rhymes or puns.

____ 32 I like to observe things closely and keep detailed records.

____ 33 I can double or triple a cooking recipe or carpentry measurement in my head.

____ 34 I often have a tune in my head.

____ 35 Other people sometimes ask me to explain the meaning of words I use.

____ 36 I enjoy solving jigsaw puzzles, mazes, or other visual puzzles.

____ 37 I feel comfortable in a crowd.

____ 38 I beat my friends in chess, checkers or other strategy games.

____ 39 I know a lot about biology, rocks or stars.

____ 40 I frequently use hand gestures or other forms of body language when conversing.

Aim

This activity helps students apply their knowledge of Multiple Intelligences in order to study more effectively. It is designed to be done after an introduction to Multiple Intelligences, eg Activity 18.

To the teacher

Make one copy of the worksheet and answer the questions about yourself as a learner.

What do you learn about yourself? How do your learning preferences influence your teaching? Does your teaching style take account of the learning preferences of others?

Consider different students you know (particularly students you might consider 'difficult') and try to answer the questions from their point of view. Consider these answers in relation to your teaching style.

Decide how to exploit the activity most effectively with your students.

Method

1   Give one copy of the worksheet to each student. They work in pairs through the first section, asking each other the statements as questions and filling in the form for their partner. They decide together which intelligence they think each question refers to.

At lower language levels, work on question formation before leaving students to work in pairs.

2   Students work in small groups to complete the second part of the worksheet, which asks them to consider ways of using different intelligences and to formulate suggestions.

3   In their groups, students discuss which strategies they already use and identify new strategies they might like to try.

Optional follow up

Set four or five short and very different exercises for homework: a piece of creative writing, a short translation, a mini-project (eg find ten labels in English in the supermarket), two grammar exercises, one easy, one difficult, etc. Tell students that you will not primarily mark the homework for achievement. They should use the opportunity to discover which strategies they would naturally use with each exercise, and then to try different strategies.

The following day, students discuss and compare the strategies they used for each task and try to identify those which seemed most effective.

Remind them that the aim is to find more strategies to help them learn effectively. There is not one right answer – nor is there necessarily the same right answer for each person, nor the same right answer for one person in every situation. Effective people have a range of strategies to choose from.

Ask students to write down ten specific things they can (and will!) do to improve their study habits using different intelligences.

Level   ✳ ✳

Key

1	Bodily-Kinaesthetic	9	Bodily-Kinaesthetic
2	Linguistic	10	Logical-Mathematical
3	Intrapersonal	11	Naturalist
4	Logical-Mathematical	12	Musical
5	Naturalist	13	Intrapersonal
6	Spatial-Visual	14	Linguistic
7	Interpersonal	15	Interpersonal
8	Musical	16	Spatial-Visual

Suggestions for making the most of each intelligence when studying are:

Linguistic Make notes, or try speaking aloud.

Logical-Mathematical Try to bring in numbers, calculations, logic, classifications or critical thinking skills.

Spatial-Visual Use visual aids, visualisation, colour, art or metaphor.

Musical Play music while you work, put a rhythmic or melodic framework onto key points.

Bodily-Kinaesthetic Try to involve your whole body or get hands-on experiences.

Intrapersonal Work quietly alone, incorporate personal memories, give yourself choices.

Interpersonal Try to work with other people, to discuss and share ideas.

Naturalist Do your thinking in the fresh air, surrounded by trees. Try to sort things into categories as much as possible.

✔ CONSIDER your own study habits by looking at the following statements relating to Multiple Intelligences. Tick the relevant boxes and identify the intelligence.

Always Sometimes Never Type of intelligence

When you are doing homework:

1 You feel it. You do something active.

2 You talk it through in your head.

3 You find what is most meaningful.

4 You analyse it.

5 You concentrate on the details.

6 You try to see it.

7 You talk it through with someone.

8 You set rhythm to it.

When you don't understand something:

9 You walk around and move your hands.

10 You define the problem and work on it logically.

11 You go outside into a park or garden.

12 You put on relaxing music or sing the problem.

13 You go off by yourself to find the key to it.

14 You repeat, or rephrase, to understand the words.

15 You work through it with a partner.

16 You picture it and re-picture it, or draw it.

SUGGEST ways of making the most of each intelligence when you are studying.

Linguistic

Logical-Mathematical

Spatial-Visual

Musical

Bodily-Kinaesthetic

Interpersonal

Intrapersonal

Naturalist

Aim

This is a story to get students thinking about the roles people play in life.

To the teacher

Before you look at the Notes, read the story yourself and answer the question, *'Which character do you sympathise with most – the farmer, the biologist or the eagle?'*

Read the Notes. What do you learn about yourself? Is it accurate?

Decide how to exploit the activity most effectively with your students.

Method

1   Give one copy of the worksheet to each student. Read the story aloud, expressively, to the students as they read the text.

2   In small groups, students tell one another which character they sympathised with (liked) most, and why.

3   Tell students about the life roles and ask them to continue their discussion.

4   The story is a 'melodrama', because the characters are wooden and stereotyped: the farmer was always the persecutor, the biologist was always the rescuer, and the eagle was always the victim. In real life (and in more subtle drama), people can take different roles in different situations, and people can change.

5   Ask students to continue the story (either in class or as homework) in such a way that the characters change their roles. Maybe the eagle becomes a rescuer or a persecutor, the farmer becomes a victim or a rescuer, and the biologist becomes a persecutor or a victim.

6   In small groups, students talk about drama they have seen recently (TV soap operas, movies, plays) – what happened and which roles people were playing.

7   Students move into new small groups. They discuss times and situations in their lives when they play (or played) the role of persecutor, victim and rescuer. Which role do they play most often?

    (Remind students that they only have to share things about themselves which they are comfortable about others knowing.)

8   Discuss with students how they can break out of playing one of these three roles, and whether there are other roles people play in life.

Optional follow up

Students write about a time when they played one of the roles in life. It can be done either as a story, a newspaper account or a short play.

Level   ✳

Notes

One view of people is that they tend to play one of three roles in life: the Persecutor, the Victim or the Rescuer.

If you sympathise most with the biologist, you think of yourself as one of life's rescuers. You rescue people (even if sometimes they don't want to be rescued!).

If you sympathise most with the farmer, you think of yourself as one of life's persecutors. You make things happen.

If you sympathise most with the eagle, you think of yourself as one of life's victims. Things are always happening to you.

THE EAGLE

Once there was a farmer who was out one day when he saw an eagle. 'Mm,' he thought, 'that big bird would make a tasty meal.' So he shot it – bang! The eagle fell through the air and landed heavily on the ground.

But when the farmer saw the eagle's big beak and sharp talons, he thought, 'That bird's a killer. Ugh! I don't want to eat something that's been killing animals and eating meat.' Then the farmer had an idea. He climbed high, high up the cliff until he found the eagle's nest. And in the eagle's nest was the eagle's egg, still warm.

So the farmer carried the eagle's egg to the farmhouse, and put it under a hen with her other eggs. And after some time, the little eagle chick hatched along with the baby chickens. The eagle chick grew up in the farmyard among the chickens. And the eagle thought it was a chicken. And it learnt to peck corn, just like the chickens.

And the baby eagle grew, and grew, and grew, until, when it stretched its wings, they were two metres from tip to tip, and the feathers were a beautiful golden brown colour. But still the eagle thought it was a chicken, and it pecked the corn just like the chickens.

And the farmer looked at the eagle and said 'Mm! This eagle is getting very big. It will make a tasty meal, and this eagle has never eaten meat.' So the farmer starting sharpening his knife – scritch! swish! scritch! swish!

A biologist who was walking past the farmyard saw the magnificent young eagle pecking corn among the chickens. 'Hello,' he said. 'What are you doing in a farmyard? You're not a chicken, you're an eagle.'

So saying, the biologist lifted up the eagle and threw it into the air, but the eagle fell to the ground and once again started pecking the corn among the chickens.

Just then the farmer came out of the farmhouse with his sharp, sharp knife ready to kill the eagle for his supper.

The biologist picked up the eagle again, lifted it high in the air and ran down the field, shouting, 'You are an eagle, not a chicken.' The eagle, to balance, spread forth one wing and then the other. 'Fly, eagle, fly,' shouted the biologist, and he threw the eagle into the air.

The eagle glided gently back to the ground, and then walked back to the farmyard and pecked the corn among the chickens.

The farmer walked towards the eagle with his sharp, sharp knife, and he put out his hand to take the eagle by the neck ... but ... the biologist grabbed the eagle and started running. The farmer ran after him, shouting, 'Stop thief. Bring back my eagle. Bring back my dinner. I've fed that eagle since it was a baby chick. It's mine!'

The biologist ran and ran and ran. He ran up the high, high cliff carrying the eagle, which by now was very heavy and seemed to be getting heavier by the minute. The farmer was following behind.

Eventually, just as the farmer was about to catch them, they reached the top of the high, high cliff. 'It's now or never,' whispered the biologist, and he threw the eagle over the cliff shouting, 'Fly! You are not a chicken. You're an eagle!'

The eagle fell through the air like a stone. Then, to balance, it spread out its wings, and the rising warm air caught it and held it in mid-air. And then the warm air lifted the eagle and it began to rise higher and higher and higher, until it was soaring high in the sky. Then, for the first time in its life, it flapped its wings and began to fly.

And from that day on, the eagle lived as an eagle, flying and soaring high in the sky.

But sometimes in its heart there was a great loneliness and a great sadness. Sometimes in its heart it was a chicken who longed to return to the farmyard and be among the chickens pecking corn.

Aim

This activity helps students visualise and attain their ideal future.

To the teacher

Make one copy of the worksheet and fill it in for yourself. You might do it about your life as a whole, or focus specifically on one aspect – your personal life, teaching, a leisure activity.

Decide how to exploit the activity most effectively with your students.

Method

1 If you want to add anything to the worksheet, make one copy first, make your changes and then make a copy for each student.

2 Students sit quietly in their own space, possibly with eyes closed, possibly with gentle music playing. Ask them to imagine their lives one week into the future ... one month into the future ... one year into the future ... five years into the future ... ten years into the future. (Leave about 20 seconds between the different times, and possibly alter the time scales depending on the age of the students and when they are likely to be making life-changing decisions.) Ask them: Where will they be? What would they like to be doing? What kind of life will they be living? What kind of job would they like to have? Or what studies will they be doing?

3 Give out one copy each of the worksheet and ask them to work individually and write down their answers to each specific question about the future.

4 In small groups, students discuss their dreams and their answers to the questions. Which questions did they find easy to answer? Which ones were difficult? Which ones had they never thought of before?

5 Read out the information about Gregory Bateson's work (see Notes). Ask students the questions about their values and beliefs, and give them time to consider and discuss each question in small groups.

6 Students read through the answers to their questions about the future again and make any changes they want to make. They then write a series of actions that they can take – now – to start them on the path to their ideal future.

Level ✳ ✳

Notes

Gregory Bateson looked very carefully at the questions Where, When, What, How, Why, Who. His analysis is widely used in business and sociological studies, and it has been incorporated into Neuro-Linguistic Programming, initially by Robert Dilts.

Where? When? = Environmental Constraints (relatively easy to change)

What? = Behaviour or Actions (easy to change)

How? = Capabilities or Direction (more difficult to change)

Why? = Beliefs, Values, Permission, Motivation (difficult to change, especially if you are not consciously aware of them)

Who? = Identity, Mission (difficult to change)

Ask yourself how much your behaviour depends on your beliefs and values. Could you work as a paid murderer? Could you live as a beggar on the streets? If you had different beliefs about yourself, could you become more capable?

In experiments, classes of learners with higher expectations develop higher competence. Classes of learners with low expectations develop low competence. If other people had higher expectations of you, would you become more competent? Do your own expectations affect your friends and family – or yourself?

What are your beliefs about yourself and the world? How have your beliefs about yourself been formed? Many people model themselves on significant others, ie they try to be like their father/mother/teacher/gang leader. Other beliefs come from repetitive experiences, which may be positive or negative. Other beliefs are from your culture or environment.

Think about what you expect or hope to be doing in ten years' time. What sort of job or studies do you want to be doing? (If you don't know what you *do* want, identify some of the things you *don't* want.) Answer the following questions.

WHERE? Which places, countries, situations do you want (or not want) to be in?

_____

_____

WHAT? What do you want to do or not do? How do you want to behave? How don't you want to behave?

_____

_____

WHEN? What things do you want to be doing at what times of the day, week, month or year?

_____

_____

HOW? What existing skills would you like to use more? What extra skills would you like to have?

_____

_____

WHY? Why do you do what you do? What are your beliefs and values? What beliefs and values are you prepared to change, and which do you feel you want to keep?

_____

_____

WHO? What sort of person are you? What matters most to you? Which things about yourself are you prepared to change and which things do you want to stay the same?

_____

_____

What actions can you take now to make your ideal future come into being?

_____

_____

Aim

This activity helps students realise their dreams.

To the teacher

Make one copy of the worksheet and fill it in for yourself. You might have some personal dreams you want to fulfil, but you might also like to think about your dreams for your students and your own development as a teacher. Sit quietly with some music playing (something classical and calming, eg by Bach or Pachelbel) as you doodle (using your right brain). Then use your left brain, in the second half of the activity, to think more logically about how you can make your dream come true.

Decide how to exploit the activity most effectively with your students.

Method

1   Do the activity with your students as described above. Give them each a copy of the worksheet and preferably make available a range of coloured pens or crayons. Say that they'll have about 15 minutes to complete the first part of the task, so they might like to sit and listen to the music for a few minutes and just let their minds wander before they start drawing. Ask them to work quietly, alone, without talking, as you play the music.

2   Students talk together in pairs or small groups to 'analyse' and interpret one another's pictures.

3   They work in pairs on the second part of the activity. They explain the dream they have chosen to work on and help each other come up with objections and counter-objections.

4   Make sure that everyone has written the three actions they can take now. Everyone stands up, and speaking all together, loudly (so in fact no-one will hear what anyone else says), they say the first action they will take. Then, on your count, everyone says their second action – and their third. The aim of this, of course, is not that they communicate their decisions to other people, but that they actually say them out loud so that the decisions take on a kind of exterior reality.

Level   *

Notes

Students might have a clear idea of what their own symbols and doodles mean as they draw them, but they might still gain some surprising insights if their pictures are 'interpreted' by someone else.

The following should not be taken too seriously, but might give them some ideas to get them talking:

thick, strong lines – positive intention

thin, weak lines – indecision, lack of commitment or clarity

closed doodles, eg spiralling inwards – introspection

lines pointing out, eg starburst – extrovert, open to others, outward looking

large sweeping lines – a general overview, the big picture

lots of small doodles – specific details, but possible lack of clarity about how they fit together

This page is for you to dream how you would like your future to be.

First cover the writing at the bottom of the page with a sheet of clean paper. Then start daydreaming. Just let your mind wander and, when you're ready, use this space to draw pictures, symbols or doodles to represent your future.

Look at what you have drawn and 'analyse' it with a partner.
Then write about a dream.

This is my dream _____

THREE reasons why this dream can't come true

A _____

B _____

C _____

TWO ways to overcome each of the objections

A 1 _____

A 2 _____

B 1 _____

B 2 _____

C 1 _____

C 2 _____

THREE things I can and will do NOW to start making my dream come true

I will _____

I will _____

I will _____

Aim

This is a free-standing activity which can be done at any time to stimulate students to think and talk about their priorities in life.

To the teacher

Before you read the Notes, follow the instructions on the worksheet and draw the symbols yourself. Then read the Notes and interpret what you have drawn. What do you think your drawings show about you? How accurate do you think this is?

Decide how to exploit the activity most effectively with your students.

Method

1   If you want to add anything to the worksheet, make one copy first, make your changes, and then make a copy for each student.

2   Before you hand out the worksheet, brainstorm vocabulary relating to different shapes and prepositions, writing the words up on the board.

3   Give one copy of the worksheet to each student and read aloud both sets of instructions, giving students time to draw each time. Students work individually.

4   In small groups, they share their drawings and talk about the differences and similarities between what they have drawn.

5   Tell students what the shapes and patterns 'mean', and give them time to talk in their groups.

6   In new groups, students discuss their 'meanings' and ask the question, *'Is it true about me?'*

7   At the end of the activity, students fill in the 'word storm' box on their worksheets, either by copying from the board, or by trying to remember (while facing in the opposite direction) and then checking with the words on the board.

Optional follow up

Students write about themselves, eg in a letter to a penfriend, incorporating the information in this exercise.

Level ✳

Notes

☐   The square relates to the world, the outside world

◯   The circle is to do with home, your home, your house.

△   The triangle stands for you, yourself, your ego, your direction in life.

ω   The double-u is **sex**.

Usually people draw something bigger and more central if it is important to them. In western culture people usually draw the past to the left and the future up and to the right. (For left-handed people it may be the opposite.)

Ask students which symbol is most important for them. What is the relationship between the symbols? Which direction are you going in: towards home, the world, or sex?

These interpretations should not be taken too seriously. They are just for fun and to get students talking. However, they can often give remarkably accurate insights.

1 Draw the four shapes as big or as small as you would like them, putting them in any order, facing in any direction. Make any changes you want.

2 Now draw the four shapes TOGETHER in any way you choose: any size, one inside the other, on top of each other, underneath, overlapping, etc.

WORD STORM

Write down words to describe shapes and words for showing the relationship of things to each another. Here are some to get you started.

SHAPES	RELATIONSHIPS	
a circle	above	touching
circular	near	bigger than
round	in the middle	half the size of

Aim

This activity helps students explore how it feels to listen and be listened to – or not. The long-term benefit is to set up some class rules to encourage students to listen respectfully to one another.

To the teacher

Make two copies of the worksheet and do the activity with a friend or colleague. What do you find difficult? What do you find easy? What are the benefits and drawbacks of the different kinds of listening?

Compare your rules for good listening with the information on empathetic listening (see Notes).

What advantages would there be if students always listened in this way in class? What is your natural style when you are listening to students? Could you improve on your listening style?

Decide how to exploit the activity most effectively with your students.

Method

1 If you want to add anything to the worksheet, make a copy of it first, make your changes, then make copies for the students.

2 Students freely choose a partner. Each pair sits away from other pairs. One student is A, the other B.

3 Each student gets a worksheet and thinks of an easy topic to talk about, eg a hobby, a holiday, something interesting that happened.

4 A gets ready to talk. B gets ready to ignore A. A talks, B ignores A for two minutes. As and Bs change roles.

5 Students individually write down their reactions to how it felt to ignore and be ignored, and then in small groups they discuss the experience so far.

6 A and B get ready to compete, not by shouting, but by monopolising the conversation and interrupting, rather than listening to the other person. Both try to speak as much as possible. They start talking and compete for two minutes.

7 Students write down their reactions, and then in small groups they discuss the experience so far – including the differences between ignoring and competing. Which was better?

8 As and Bs experiment with other ways of listening and write notes on their experience. Students move round into lots of different small groups and share their new experiences.

9 Groups write their rules for 'good listening'. All the ideas are put up on the wall for everyone to see.

10 Explain the rules for empathetic listening and ask students to experiment. Afterwards they write notes about the experience.

11 The class works together to propose and write down the rules of good listening that they would like to follow in lessons from now on. The rules are written out neatly and put on the classroom wall.

Level   ✳ ✳

Notes

The empathetic listener listens attentively without interrupting, maintaining eye contact and showing interest through body language.

The listener stops the speaker every 60 seconds and summarises what the speaker has said. The listener offers no conversation or opinion. The summary is to check that what the listener thinks he/she has heard is what the speaker thinks he/she has said.

Ask clarification questions only when you don't understand. (*'Do you know what I think?'* and *'Shall I tell you what happened to me?'* are not clarification questions!)

Language

The following language might be useful. Add any other words or phrases you would like to remember.

Uh huh, mmm, yes, I see …

I felt … when you …

Nobody ever listens to me!

I realise I don't usually listen to other people.

You speak and I'll listen.

Now it's my turn.

So what you're saying is …

Could you say that again? I didn't understand.

With your partner, take turns in telling a short anecdote while the other person practises the different kinds of listening. Make notes about your different experiences.

IGNORING

How it feels to ignore the speaker

_____
_____
_____

How it feels to be ignored

_____
_____
_____

COMPETING

How it feels to compete

_____
_____
_____

How it feels to be competed with

_____
_____
_____

EMPATHETIC LISTENING

How it feels to listen empathetically

_____
_____
_____

How it feels to be listened to empathetically

_____
_____
_____

RULES FOR GOOD LISTENING

1 _____
2 _____
3 _____
4 _____
5 _____

Aim

This activity encourages students to present a point of view, while challenging them to think about their beliefs about human nature.

To the teacher

Read each group of statements, imagine that you agree with them and write notes to say why you agree. Be prepared to help students fully understand each point of view even if they don't agree with it. Think where you stand and what you believe. Does your behaviour as a teacher in the classroom reflect what you believe about human nature?

Method

1   Read through these steps, decide how you are going to organise your discussion and then make the copies of the worksheets and cut them up as needed.

2   Students will be either A or B and will only see their own notes. Put all the As together and give them the A-1 statements, and all the Bs together, with the B-1 statements. Give them five minutes to think of arguments to support 'their' point of view.

3   Students get into pairs or small groups including both As and Bs. They argue that they are right and try to persuade others to change their point of view.

4   After a few minutes, students express what they really think and feel.

5   One wall in the room represents A's point of view and the opposite wall represents B's point of view. Students stand on the line between the two walls in a place which represents their own point of view – either strongly at one end or the other, or somewhere less extreme nearer the middle.

6   Ask students how many of them agree with the view they were given. How much was their opinion affected by being given a view which they spent time preparing?

7   Students change roles. Give out the A-2 statements to the new As and the B-2 statements to the new Bs. After a few minutes' preparation, they discuss the statements in small groups, strongly defending their new point of view.

8   Students place themselves on the continuum again. Have they changed their point of view at all?

Level   ✳ ✳

> ### Notes
>
> Some points for discussion are
>
> How do organisations reflect how people are? Consider:
>
> • a school
>
> • a sports club
>
> • a family
>
> • a country (the government).
>
> Are all organisations the same? What happens when one person's view of people is different from the view held by the organisation? Do they adapt? Does the organisation adapt? What are the conflicts? What are the consequences?
>
> How do these questions affect the learning that takes place at school?

(A-1) STATEMENTS

This is your point of view. Argue this view very strongly.

- Human beings are naturally lazy and reluctant to work.
- If left alone, people will do nothing useful or constructive.
- In order to get people to work and to do things which are useful and constructive, people need to be told what to do, made to do it, and supervised while they do it.
- In order to make people do things, you often have to use force, or punishment, or the fear of force or punishment. Fear is the most effective motivation.

(B-1) STATEMENTS

This is your point of view. Argue this view very strongly.

- Human beings are naturally curious, exploratory and eager to be active.
- If left alone, people are creative, imaginative and co-operative.
- The best way to achieve useful and constructive things is to allow people to participate in planning work in their own way and in their own time.
- Using force or punishment only robs people of their natural curiosity, exploration and activeness. Fear robs people of creativity, imagination and their natural desire to co-operate.

(A-2) STATEMENTS

This is your point of view. Argue this view very strongly.

- Society needs to be organised with rewards and punishments, carrots and sticks, so everyone knows exactly what he or she must do in every situation.
- Rules must be universal and clearly stated, and enforced.
- Change should come from the top down, ie from leaders who have the knowledge and understanding to make the changes which are needed.

(B-2) STATEMENTS

This is your point of view. Argue this view very strongly.

- Society without leaders is natural and just. Each person is equal and should have equal power. When people are equal, they naturally co-operate.
- Each community in each situation is capable of making its own rules and using them flexibly.
- Change should come from the bottom up, ie from the people of the community who will have to live with the changes, not from the leaders.

Aim

This activity helps students think about their strengths and weaknesses when working with others.

To the teacher

Make a copy of the worksheet and answer the questions yourself.

What do you learn about yourself as a member of a team? How do you work best with others? Do others find it easy to work with you? What kinds of people do you like to work with?

Consider your answers in relation to yourself as a teacher. Are there any ways in which you view your students as part of your team?

Decide how to exploit this activity most effectively with your students.

Method

1   If you want to add anything to the worksheet, make one copy first, make your changes, and then make a copy for each student.

2   Give each student a copy of the worksheet and talk to them about your own preferences. (Perhaps ask them to guess what you wrote.)

3   In small groups, students talk about their experiences of teamwork – their disasters and their successes.

4   In their groups, students produce a definition of a 'saboteur' and what it is they do to ruin a team. Groups report back to the class.

5   In their groups, students produce guidelines for 'an ideal team'. Everyone looks at the different guidelines produced and compares them with the information in the Notes.

6   Students work in pairs (A and B) to complete the worksheet. A asks B the question and fills in B's sheet – and vice versa.

7   Each student individually writes on a new sheet of paper (in letters big enough for others to read easily) a definition of his/her preferred role in a team.

8   Students then negotiate with others in the class to produce ideal teams of five. This is a class task, so it may be that the final group to form is not ideal, so they may need to swap places with people who have already formed a group.

9   The class then discusses how well (or not) they have been working as teams during this activity. Have they learnt any lessons about working with others?

10 Ask them how they would like to form groups in class in future: according to who they're sitting near, self-selected, teacher-imposed, with thoughtful negotiation (as in this activity) to form 'ideal' teams, working with people who they find difficult (for practice) – or possibly in different ways on different occasions.

Level   ✳ ✳

Notes

It is generally considered that a good team consists of a mixture of people who, between all of them, are able to:

• generate ideas

• lead

• do the work

• have specialist knowledge

• like to find out information

• pay attention to detail

• look after the other people in the team

• keep people focused on the task

The roles people play in their everyday lives can indicate what sort of role they are likely to play in a team. (People can play more than one role in a team.) People are different. They have different skills and enjoy taking different roles in groups.

A team might fail because it does not contain a good balance of people with the right balance of skills.

It might also fail because of the presence of a 'saboteur', who may be actively trying to destroy the task or even the team. Often, however, they don't do this deliberately. They may be in need of attention or feel undervalued, or they may have had the task imposed on them or simply not be interested in it.

1   If you join a committee, which role do you prefer?

☐ Treasurer   ☐ Chairman/chairwoman

☐ Secretary   ☐ Ordinary member

2   If you are involved in a sport, which role do you prefer?

☐ Captain   ☐ Star   ☐ Coach

☐ Referee/umpire   ☐ Social organiser ☐ Ordinary team member

☐ Fan club member   ☐ Ordinary spectator

3   If you are involved in a social event, which role do you prefer?

☐ Up-front organiser ☐ Serving drinks/food ☐ Back-room organiser

☐ Disc jockey   ☐ Cleaner   ☐ Ordinary participant

4   If you are among a group of friends, which role do you prefer?

☐ Leader   ☐ One among equals ☐ Protester

☐ Follower   ☐ Loner   ☐ Supporter of the leader

5   When you have a conversation, which role do you prefer?

☐ Talker   ☐ Commentator   ☐ Listener

☐ Interrupter   ☐ Non-participant

6   Which word or phrase do you prefer to use?

☐ 'Yes'   ☐ 'No'

☐ 'Maybe'   ☐ 'I don't know'

7   What do you like and dislike about   _____
     being part of a team?   _____

8   What strengths and skills do you   _____
     have which are useful in teamwork?   _____

9   What weaknesses do you have   _____
     when working in a team?   _____

10   What other types of people do you need _____
     to work with you to make a good team? _____
     Define the five roles which you feel   _____
     make a good team.   _____
     Which one of the five are you?   _____

Aim

This activity encourages students to understand their motivation to work and to realise the value of the contribution they and others can make to groupwork.

To the teacher

Make one copy of the worksheet and check which statements are true about you.

Compare your answers with the key (on page 64). What do you learn about yourself as a member of a team? Is this relevant to your teaching? Do you consider your students to be part of your team?

Decide how to exploit the activity most effectively with your students.

NB You will probably want to photocopy the key to give to the students.

Method

1   Students work in groups to complete the worksheet. Allow each group to have a dictionary and encourage them to read sentences aloud and check any vocabulary they don't know. Students mark their own worksheet individually.

2   Give a copy of the key to each group. Do they agree with what it says?

3   Ask groups to give a name to each type of team member. Share these as a whole class – possibly by asking groups to suggest their names, in any order, while others guess which types they refer to.

4   Ask students to evaluate their own performance in any group activities you have done recently in class.

Optional follow up

Give the class a language task which requires them to work in groups (possibly one of the early activities from this book). Put them in groups of six or seven and make it competitive by saying that the winners will be the first group where everyone has completed the task.

When the activity has ended and winners have been decided, ask them to evaluate their performance as group members. Did they act as they thought they would? Did this teamwork activity accurately predict how they would behave? Did they answer the questions honestly?

Level ✳ ✳ ✳

Notes

Possible names for team types are:

2, 11, 20	Researcher
3, 12, 21	Leader, organiser
4, 13, 22	Completer, achiever
5, 14, 23	Quality controller, detail person
6, 15, 24	People person, pacifier
7, 16, 25	Precision person
8, 17, 26	Expert, specialist
9, 18, 27	Worker

The photocopiable key for this activity is on page 64.

Put numbers in the boxes next to the statements which best describe you as a member of a team.

3 = very much me   2 = quite me   1 = a bit me   0 = not me at all

1 I work best if I can start the idea, inspire others and have autonomy.

2 I work best if I can have time to find out about the resources we all need, then tell the others.

3 I like to lead the group or bring people together into teams.

4 Give me a problem to solve and a deadline to meet.

5 I'm good at summarising progress and producing interim and final reports.

6 I love groupwork. I love sharing and fitting in with other people.

7 I like to tie up the loose ends, to dot the 'i's and cross the 't's.

8 Just ask me questions when you want to know about something in my field. Otherwise, don't bother me.

9 Don't waste my time. I'll find my task and I'll get on with it.

10 I'm motivated if I can say 'I'm the first person ever to do this in this way'.

11 I'm motivated if I can say 'What have I got? What is available?' Then I can organise the resources.

12 I like to link up and relate together what I know and what I can find out.

13 Vague ideas frustrate me. I need to make things more definite.

14 I like to comment on what I've learned, put it in order, and find what is missing.

15 I like to work in groups. My work is only one piece of the jigsaw puzzle.

16 I like my work to be thorough and look good. My problem is getting started.

17 Work? If I'm not interested, I can't do it. If I'm interested, I'll do it in great detail. You can't expect me to be interested in what I'm not interested in.

18 I work quickly and effectively. I tell myself 'That's what I've got to do' and I get on and do it.

19 I don't want one job. I like to set up new things and leave when I get bored, so I can go and start something else.

20 I want a job where I can find out 'What and where'. I like other people to use what I have found.

21 I need to be a part of a harmonious team, helping people and resources to join up. Together we are more than the sum of our parts.

22 I need to be in control to make order out of chaos.

23 I would like to work in quality control, making sure the right items are observed, analysed and reported on.

24 It's people who matter. It's the way we work rather than the particular job. I'd hate to work alone, or in a job where people can't or won't work together.

25 I need to work with people who care about the finished, final product. Don't rush me. Don't accept low standards. It must be right.

26 I want to concentrate on my subject. I'm an expert. Let me be an expert.

27 I need to be free to be effective. I need clear instructions and no obstacles. Then I work really well.

KEY TO TEAMWORK ACTIVITY

Circle any numbers for which you put 2 or 3. Then read those categories for which you have circled two or three numbers. Do you think they describe you?

1   10   19

Strengths You are an ideas person who likes to get new things started. You get fired with enthusiasm and can be inspiring to others.

Weaknesses You tend to 'run out of steam' once the first flush of enthusiasm has passed. You want to get on with the job, and get bored or give up when you meet obstacles. You rarely finish jobs and have no patience with details.

2   11   20

Strengths You love research. You love getting together all the equipment needed for a job and keeping it organised. You're good at setting up systems and keeping them going.

Weaknesses You sometimes find it hard to focus on the aim of the job. The process is often more important to you than the result.

3   12   21

Strengths You are a people person. You like organising people and working with people. You are the person who organises the group and helps people decide who's going to do what.

Weaknesses Sometimes other people can find you bossy. You are sometimes more interested in the working process and the working relationships than in the actual product or task.

4   13   22

Strengths You are very good at focusing on the task and the end product and making sure that it happens. You are good at prioritising and holding the whole project in your head when other people sometimes get lost in the details.

Weaknesses You find it hard to get down to work until everything has been sorted out and finalised. Sometimes you're better at organising the work rather than doing it.

5   14   23

Strengths You are very good at keeping the group focused on the task and the target. You are also the one who makes sure that the finished product is high quality and that the task is completed on time.

Weaknesses You prefer overseeing the work to actually doing it. You are not really an ideas person – you prefer making other people's ideas happen.

6   15   24

Strengths You are a great person to work with. You do your own work and also make sure that everyone around you is able to get on with theirs. And everyone's delighted that you remembered to bring along drinks and biscuits!

Weaknesses You do not work so well when there is conflict between different members of the group. You like everyone to get on and sometimes you put your effort into sorting out other people's problems rather than getting on with your own work.

7   16   25

Strengths You are the person who makes sure that the job gets done properly. You are prepared to go over and over something until it's right. Others rely on you to make sure that the job goes out looking good.

Weaknesses Sometimes you find it hard to see the wood for the trees – you lose sight of the target and get bogged down in the details. You often feel the need to correct other people when you hear them being imprecise or careless.

8   17   26

Strengths You are the person everyone calls on for specific help about your pet subjects. You are (and like to be known as) the specialist, the expert. You are very good at what you do.

Weaknesses You are not always too keen on doing the hard work – you prefer to give advice to others. You do not like working on projects in which other people know more than you do, and occasionally you have been known to pretend you have more expertise than you actually have.

9   18   27

Strengths Someone's got to get on and actually do the work, and it's you! You are tireless. Everyone depends on you to complete mammoth tasks in a ridiculously short time and you've never let them down yet!

Weaknesses You can be a bit impatient with people who want to talk about what's to be done rather than getting on and doing it. Remember that the initial planning stage is also important. Sometimes in the past you have done quite a lot of work on a project, only to find that you have been working in the wrong direction.